Hebraica veritas versus
Septuaginta auctoritatem

"Ignacio Carbajosa provides an excellent introduction into ancient church controversies around the need for a Scripture translation into Latin by Jerome and into its subsequent canonicity and the modern repercussions. The ancient documents have been thoroughly researched, are presented in a lively fashion, and give the reader, expert, and layman alike, much food for thought."

—EMANUEL TOV,
professor of Bible, The Hebrew University of Jerusalem

"Taking as his starting point the rivalry between Jerome's *hebraica veritas* and Augustine's *Septuaginta auctoritas*, Ignacio Carbajosa skillfully illustrates how, mutatis mutandis, the tension between the two positions still exists in modern biblical scholarship. The synthesis which he suggests happens also to be of particular relevance for biblical translations used in liturgical worship. This is a highly illuminating and most welcome discussion."

—SEBASTIAN P. BROCK,
emeritus reader in Syriac studies, University of Oxford

"Modern Christians face many options for a Bible. Which is the right one? The same question confronted Jerome and Augustine, two giants of early Christian theology who discussed this matter and came to different conclusions. This slender volume enables us to listen in on their conversation. Approaching the matter from a Roman Catholic perspective, Ignacio Carbajosa provides expert guidance through the maze of issues posed by this wonderful book's title."

—EDMON L. GALLAGHER,
professor of Christian Scripture, Heritage Christian University

"For the Church, does scriptural authority lie in the Hebrew text of the Old Testament, or in the ancient Greek Septuagint translation? This is a wonderfully clear and accessible exposition of the debate first initiated by St. Augustine and St. Jerome, and why it mattered both then and now. Aimed at an educated readership in Catholic circles, the book will also be of interest to anyone involved in biblical studies."

—ALISON SALVESEN,
professor of early Judaism and Christianity, University of Oxford

Hebraica veritas versus Septuaginta auctoritatem

Does a Canonical Text
of the Old Testament Exist?

IGNACIO CARBAJOSA

Translated by Paul Stevenson
Foreword by Adrian Schenker

◆PICKWICK *Publications* • Eugene, Oregon

HEBRAICA VERITAS VERSUS SEPTUAGINTA AUCTORITATEM
Does a Canonical Text of the Old Testament Exist?

Copyright © 2024 Ignacio Carbajosa. All rights reserved. Except for brief quotations in critical publications or reviews, no part of this book may be reproduced in any manner without prior written permission from the publisher. Write: Permissions, Wipf and Stock Publishers, 199 W. 8th Ave., Suite 3, Eugene, OR 97401.

Pickwick Publications
An Imprint of Wipf and Stock Publishers
199 W. 8th Ave., Suite 3
Eugene, OR 97401

www.wipfandstock.com

PAPERBACK ISBN: 978-1-6667-7494-8
HARDCOVER ISBN: 978-1-6667-7495-5
EBOOK ISBN: 978-1-6667-7496-2

Cataloguing-in-Publication data:

Names: Carbajosa, Ignacio, 1967–, author. | Stevenson, Paul, translator. | Schenker, Adrian, foreword.

Title: Hebraica veritas versus septuaginta auctoritatem : does a canonical text of the old testament exist? / Ignacio Carbajosa ; translated by Paul Stevenson ; forword by Adrian Schenker.

Description: Eugene, OR : Pickwick Publications, 2024 | Includes bibliographical references and index.

Identifiers: ISBN 978-1-6667-7494-8 (paperback) | ISBN 978-1-6667-7495-5 (hardcover) | ISBN 978-1-6667-7496-2 (ebook)

Subjects: LCSH: Bible.—Old Testament—Versions. | Bible.—Old Testament.—Greek.—Septuagint.

Classification: BS 1177.3 .C375 2024 (paperback) | BS 1177.3 .C375 (ebook)

03/11/24

Original Spanish edition:
Hebraica veritas versus Septuaginta auctoritatem
¿Existe un texto canónico del Antiguo Testamento?
© 2021 by Ignacio Carbajosa
© 2021 by Editorial Verbo divino,
Estella (Navarra), Spain

The English translation of this work has been made possible thanks to funding from San Dámaso University (UESD- OIRI Nº Prot.: 2020-21; 2ª/3/1).

Contents

Foreword by Adrian Schenker | vii

Abbreviations | ix

Introduction: On the 16th Centenary of the Death of Saint Jerome | xv

CHAPTER 1
The Polemic between Jerome and Augustine: Should the Old Testament Be Translated from the Hebrew or from the Greek? | 1

CHAPTER 2
The Textual Differences between the Hebrew and the Greek Bibles | 10

CHAPTER 3
The *Hebraica Veritas*: Lights | 25

CHAPTER 4
The *Hebraica Veritas*: Shadows | 36

CHAPTER 5
The *Septuaginta Auctoritas*: Lights | 42

CHAPTER 6
The *Septuaginta Auctoritas*: Shadows | 65

CHAPTER 7
A Word from the Church: The Decree of Trent | 80

CHAPTER 8
The Latin Vulgate: A Work of Synthesis | 85

CHAPTER 9
Lessons from the Past for Overcoming the Polemic | 93

CHAPTER 10
The Synthetic Principle in the Liturgical Translations | 105

Bibliography | *115*

Author Index | *123*

Scripture Index | *127*

Foreword

THIS BOOK RESPONDS TO a real need of those who love the Bible and in particular the "Old Testament" or the "Hebrew Bible". These two designations are an indication of this need: what is the true or best form we would like to have for personal reading and for liturgical community proclamation? We know, of course, that a discreet and silent troop of gardeners is busy keeping the garden of the Bible in its original beauty. These are those who dedicate themselves to textual criticism.

In his short book, Ignacio Carbajosa traces the history of textual criticism in its "natural environment". It is certainly an ancient and modern science with its resources and methods often described. But its founders and first teachers in the case of the biblical books of the Holy Scriptures, the founders of the criticism of their texts, made use of critical science in the service of their faith, first Jewish, then Christian. For they wished to preserve the authenticity of the books on which their religious convictions were based and were proclaimed in synagogal worship and ecclesial liturgies, according to the custom of the different places where they were celebrated.

Carbajosa's book shows this above all for the deployment of this safeguard of a reliable biblical text in the Latin Church, in Western Europe. Here, the great scholar and translator of the Old Testament, Jerome (347-420) gave the criticism of the text of Scripture a powerful impulse, still alive to this day. He was familiar with the critical work of the Jewish rabbis produced before him and with the huge undertaking of the synopsis of the Bible in Hebrew and Greek called *Hexapla*. No one had an instrument of textual criticism of the Old Testament before this exhaustive comparison of the two texts. It was the work of Origen, the outstanding scholar of biblical studies in Alexandria and Caesarea in Palestine, a century before Jerome.

Foreword

It follows from this history of textual criticism at the origins of Christianity that it was based on the Hebrew Bible, the original of the Old Testament, and simultaneously on the Greek Bible, the oldest version translated by Jewish scholars in the third and second centuries B.C.E., called the "Septuagint." Unlike rabbinic Judaism, Scripture in Hebrew was to be read in the Church, but without abandoning the Septuagint, since the Church needed both for its prayer, preaching, and theology. Such was the conclusion of the two-century-long debate from Origen to St. Jerome and St. Augustine, the greatest textual critics and learned theologians of Christian antiquity in East and West. In different ways, they understood that the Greek-speaking and Latin-speaking churches needed these two lungs. They owed this intelligence to their detailed knowledge of Scripture ("textual criticism") and to the ecclesial practice of Christians based on these two sources, the original Hebrew text of most of the books of the Old Testament (*veritas hebraica*, as Jerome said) and the indispensable contribution of the ancient Greek Bible (the authority of the Septuagint according to Augustine's expression).

At this point, the originality of Ignacio Carbajosa's thesis becomes apparent: the situation has remained the same throughout the centuries for the Catholic Church in the West. Research into the modern history of biblical texts shows this with great clarity. (In the Syriac East as far as India, the situation would be analogous: the Hebrew Bible with the venerable Syriac Bible.) This short book in ten chapters goes through the history of the biblical text in a large fresco full of essential facts and arrives at the end, in chapter 10, at a very surprising practical conclusion. It may not be enough on its own, but it is as precise as a GPS to orient oneself: in a word: this book is a theology of biblical texts in the Catholic Church. It shows the fruit of textual work on the Old Testament for the life of the Church. "Catholic" here includes "ecumenical," for the relationship between Bibles in the plural and churches, discovered by Origen, Jerome, and Augustine in the days of the united Church, can certainly teach us even today. And since the Septuagint is no less the work of Judaism than the Rabbinic Bible, it is not rash to conclude: the Septuagint is also a precious Jewish legacy.

Adrian Schenker O.P.

Abbreviations

1. MAJOR REFERENCES WORKS

AAS	*Acta Apostolicae Sedis*
EB	*Enchiridion Biblicum. Documenta ecclesiastica Sacram Scripturam spectantia*. Auctoritate Pontificae Commissionis de Re Biblica edita. Romae: Arnodo, 1956.
HBCE	*The Hebrew Bible: A Critical Edition*
OLM	*Ordo Lectionum Missae*. Editio typica altera. Romae: Libreria Vaticana, 1981.
THB 1A	*Textual History of the Bible, The Hebrew Bible*. Vol. 1A, *Overview Articles*. Edited by Armin Lange and Emanuel Tov. Leiden: Brill, 2016
THB 1B	*Textual History of the Bible, The Hebrew Bible*. Vol. 1B, *Pentateuch, Former and Latter Prophets*. Edited by Armin Lange and Emanuel Tov. Leiden: Brill, 2017.
THB 1C	*Textual History of the Bible, The Hebrew Bible*. Vol. 1C, *The Writings*. Edited by Armin Lange and Emanuel Tov. Leiden: Brill, 2017.
THB 2B	*The Textual History of the Bible*. Vol. 2, *Deuterocanonical Scriptures*. Part 2B, *Baruch/Jeremiah, Daniel (Additions), Ecclesiasticus/Ben Sira, Enoch, Esther (Additions), Ezra*. Edited by Frank Feder and Matthias Henze. Leiden: Brill, 2019.
THB 2C	*The Textual History of the Bible*. Vol. 2, *Deuterocanonical Scriptures*. Part 2C, *Jubilees, Judith, Maccabees, Prayer of Manasseh, Psalms 151-155, Psalms and Odes of Solomon,*

| | *Tobit, Wisdom of Solomon.* Edited by Frank Feder and Matthias Henze. Leiden: Brill, 2019. |
| THBE | *The Text of the Hebrew Bible and Its Editions: Studies in Celebration of the Fifth Centennial of the Complutensian Polyglot.* Edited by Andrés Piquer Otero and Pablo Torijano Morales. Leiden: Brill, 2017. |

2. RABBINIC WORKS

Misnah

| m. ʾAbot | Avot |

Babylonian Talmud

| b. Ber. | Berakhot |
| b. Meg. | Megillah |

Other Rabbinic Works

| Meg. Taʿan. | Megillat Taanit |
| Sep. Torah | Sefer Torah |

3. ANCIENT GREEK AND LATIN WRITINGS

Ambrose

| *Fid.* | *De fide* |
| *Spir.* | *De Spiritu Sancto* |

(Anonymous)

| *Exhort. Grae.* | *Exhortatio ad Graecos* |

(Anonymous)

Abbreviations

Let. Aris.   *Letter of Aristeas*

Augustine
C. litt. Petil.   *Contra litteras Petiliani*
Civ.   *De civitate Dei*
Doctr. chr.   *De doctrina christiana*
Enarrat. Ps.   *Enarrationes in Psalmos*
Tract. Ev. Jo.   *In Evangelium Johannis tractatus*
Trin.   *De Trinitate*

Clement of Alexandria
Strom.   *Stromata*

Epiphanius
Mens. pond.   *De Mensuris et Ponderibus*

Eusebius
Hist. eccl.   *Historia Ecclesiastica*
Praep. ev.   *Praeparatio evangelica*

Hilary
Tract. Ps.   *Tractatus super Psalmos*

Irenaeus
Haer.   *Adversus Haereses*

Abbreviations

Jerome

Complete Works	Obras Completas de San Jerónimo. Edición bilingüe promovida por la orden de San Jerónimo. 15 vols. Madrid: BAC, 1999–2015.
Letters	Epistolario. Edición bilingüe. Traducción, introducciones y notas de Juan Bautista Valero. 2 vols. Madrid: BAC, 1993–95.
Pr. Dan.	Prologue to the Book of Daniel
Pr. Ev.	Prologue to the Evangelists
Pr. Galeatus	Galeatus Prologue of Saint Jerome, Presbyter, to the Divine Books Translated by Himself from Hebrew into Latin
Pr. Isa. heb.	Prologue to the Book of the Prophet Isaiah Translated from the Hebrew
Pr. Job gr.	Prologue to the Book of Job Amended in accordance with the Greek Text
Pr. Job heb.	Prologue to the Book of Job Translated from the Hebrew
Pr. Jud.	Prologue to the Book of Judith (Obras Completas, II.481–83)
Pr. Par. gr.	Prologue to the Book of the Paralipomena Amended in Latin according to the Greek text.
Pr. Par. heb.	Prologue to the Book of the Paralipomena Translated into Latin in accordance with Hebrew Text
Pr. Pent. heb.	Prologue to the Pentateuch Translated from the Hebrew
Pr. Ps. heb.	Prologue to the Book of the Psalms according to the Hebrews
Pr. Tob.	Prologue to the Book of Tobit
Qu. hebr. Gen	Quaestionum hebraicarum liber in Genesim

John Chrysostom

Hom. Hebr.	Homiliae in epistulam ad Hebraeos

Josephus

A.J.	Antiquities of the Jews

Abbreviations

Justin

| 2 Apol. | *Apologia* II |
| Dial. | *Dialogus cum Tryphone* |

Origen

| Ep. Afr. | *Epistula ad Africanum* |
| Comm. Matt. | *Commentarius in Matthaeum* |

Philo

| Mos. | *De vita Mosis* |

4. OTHER ABBREVIATIONS

BAC	Biblioteca de Autores Cristianos
B.C.E.	Before Common Era
C.E.	Common Era
ca.	circa
cf.	confer
et al.	*et alia*
ed./eds.	editor/editors
LXX	Septuagint
MT	Masoretic Text
n.	note
NT	New Testament
OG	Old Greek
OT	Old Testament
SBL	Society of Biblical Literature
SP	Samaritan Pentateuch
v.	verse

Introduction
On the 16th Centenary of the Death of Saint Jerome

SEPTEMBER 30, 2020 WAS the 1,600th anniversary of the death of Saint Jerome, patron of those who study the Scriptures. On that very day, Pope Francis published the Apostolic Letter *Scripturae Sacrae Affectus*, commemorating "his tireless activity as a scholar, translator and exegete" and his "profound knowledge of the Scriptures, his zeal for making their teaching known, his skill as an interpreter of texts, his ardent and at times impetuous defense of Christian truth, his asceticism and harsh eremitical discipline, his expertise as a generous and sensitive spiritual guide."[1]

The enormous work of translation of the wise monk of Bethlehem, and his penetrating understanding of the Scriptures, have determined the approach to the Bible in the Christian West. It is for good reason that for centuries the Latin Church has read the Scriptures through the translation that we know as the *Vulgate*, the work of Saint Jerome. Beyond the influence which his translation had on Western language and culture, the Vulgate entailed a certain understanding of the "original" text of the Old Testament (OT). The principle of *hebraica veritas* (which could be translated, according to its sense, as "the truth comes from the Hebrew text"), which guided the work of translation of the doctor of the Church, gave an importance to the Hebrew text (in which the OT had originally been written) which it had not had until that time.

To translate the OT from its original language may today seem to us rather obvious, to the point that we take it for granted in the Bibles we use. However, in Jerome's time everything was less obvious, given the weight that the Greek version of the LXX had in the Church. Moreover, to translate the OT from the Hebrew manuscripts that were available to Jerome, and not from the "traditional" Greek text, involved a number of aporias

1. Francis, *Scripturae Sacrae Affectus*, para. 1.

Introduction

which quickly came to light in his epistolary correspondence with Saint Augustine.

Straddling the fourth and fifth centuries, the two great figures of the Latin West engaged in a dialectical battle in which we find clearly delineated the two principles which are in tension and which have determined the reception of the biblical text down to our time: the value of the "original" text (*hebraica veritas*) and the authority of the text received by the Church (*Septuaginta auctoritas*).

It is worthwhile, on the occasion of the centenary of Saint Jerome, to turn again to a matter which continues to be current and which must still be understood fairly. To this matter are related some questions which cannot be answered immediately and which are still the object of discussion: focusing only on the OT, is it possible to speak of a canonical text (not book)? If so, what might it be? In what language is that canonical text? Which passages does it include and which does it exclude? On what text should our liturgical translations be based? Can an ancient version come to be more important than the text on which it is based? Is it possible to speak of inspired translators?

Hebraica veritas versus Septuaginta auctoritatem describes the tension between two just principles which must be resolved without censuring either of them. This work, which describes the origins of the polemic, is intended to contribute to uncovering a synthetic principle which is already present in the Vulgate and in the Magisterium of the Church, and which it is worthwhile to reexamine in order not to lose the richness which the multilingual word of God has given to us.

CHAPTER 1

The Polemic between Jerome and Augustine

Should the Old Testament Be Translated from the Hebrew or from the Greek?

JEROME'S CAREER AS A TRANSLATOR

Jerome arrived in Rome in the year 382 in the company of his bishop, Paulinus of Antioch. His gifts as a man of letters and a vir trilinguis (Latin, Greek and Hebrew) even at that time caught the attention of Pope Damasus, who made him his secretary. Perhaps the most important task that he entrusted to him was that of unifying the different Latin versions of the gospels which were circulating in the Christian West by comparing them to the Greek originals and producing a single translation. In 384, the very year of the death of Saint Damasus, Jerome presented his revision to the Pope:

> You oblige me to make a new work from another one which is old, namely: that among the copies of the Scriptures dispersed throughout the whole world I should be almost like an arbiter and that, since they vary among themselves, I should decide which are those that are in agreement with the Greek truth [cum Graeca consentiant veritate].[1]

---

1. Jerome, *Pr. Ev.* (*Complete Works*, II, 509). All the texts of Saint Jerome, with the exception of the Epistolary, will be cited from the bilingual edition *Obras Completas de San Jerónimo. Edición bilingüe promovida por la orden de San Jerónimo* (from now on, *Complete Works*). The Roman numeral indicates the volume and the following one, the

Already in this prologue the elements are present which will guide Saint Jerome in the revision of the rest of the Bible. The starting point is the disparity between the Latin manuscripts of the same book, attributable to different copyists, glossers, editors, and even translators. The criterion is the pull toward the original texts, in the case of the New Testament (NT) the *Graeca veritas*.

It does not appear that the mandate of Pope Damasus extended beyond the revision of the gospels. In fact, it is doubtful whether the present Vulgate of the rest of the NT was the work of the saint from Stridon (Dalmatia). Be that as it may, when Jerome left Rome in the year 385, he was already contemplating the project of a complete revision of the Latin OT. In this case, the learned translator would face new problems: to the disparity present in the Latin manuscripts, on account of the errors which had been introduced over time, was added the fact of a larger disparity in the manuscripts of the Greek version with which the Latin would have to be compared.

Indeed, Jerome speaks of up to three different "recensions" of the Greek *Septuaginta* (LXX) version that were circulating: that of Hesychius, in Alexandria and Egypt, that of Lucian, in Antioch, and the one that was circulating in Palestine, which went back to the work of Origen and his disciples Eusebius and Pamphilus.[2] To this must be added the new Greek translations done by Aquila, Symmachus, and Theodotion. It is not surprising that Jerome wanted to bring order by doing a revision of the *Vetus Latina* of the OT on the basis of the "critical" edition of the Greek text done by Origen in the fifth column of his Hexapla. In that column, the Alexandrian had placed his edition of the LXX, marking with an obelus the words that were not found in the Hebrew manuscripts and adding, between asterisks, a Greek translation of what was missing in the Septuagint and, contrariwise, was read in the Hebrew.

From 386, when he was already settled in Bethlehem, until 390, Jerome carried out the revision of a good number of books of the Latin OT with the help of the fifth Hexaplaric column, although only the revisions of the Psalter, Job, and Song of Songs have come down to us. It was around 390

---

page. The letters from and to Jerome (including the ones that Augustine addressed to him) will be cited from *Epistolario: Edición bilingüe: Traducción, introducciones y notas de Juan Bautista Valero* (from now on: *Epistolary*) [Translator's note: The English is translated directly from the Spanish citations in order to preserve the nuances and the references to the author's original source].

2. Cf. Jerome, *Pr. Par. heb.*, (*Complete Works*, II, 473).

that there came about in Jerome a change of orientation that would mark all his subsequent translation work—a change which can be described as understandable on the basis of the work that he was doing. It should not be forgotten that the saint from Stridon was one of the few Christians versed in the Scriptures who knew the three languages involved in the processes of OT translation: Latin, Greek, and Hebrew. Indeed, as early as his passage through the desert of Chalcis (ca. 375–377), while living as a hermit, he took Hebrew lessons from a Jew who had converted to Christianity.[3] Subsequently, in Bethlehem, probably compelled by the divergences that he found in the Greek versions that were based on the Hebrew, he determined to improve and deepen his knowledge of the Semitic language, this time by paying a Jewish teacher by the name of Baranina who, as fearful as Nicodemus, gave him lessons by night.[4]

In 390 the time was ripe for the change in orientation already mentioned: Jerome abandoned the revision of the *Vetus Latina* on the basis of Greek manuscripts and decided to undertake a Latin translation *ex novo* from the Hebrew "originals." From the *Graeca veritas* of the NT to the *hebraica veritas* of the OT:

> In the same way that, in the New Testament, whenever a difficulty arises among the Latins and there is a discrepancy among the codices, we resort to the spring of the Greek, in which the new Instrument is written, so also, with respect to the Old Testament, when there are discrepancies between Greeks and Latins, we turn to the Hebrew original (*ad Hebraicam confugimus veritatem*), such that what comes out of the spring, this is what we have to seek in the streams.[5]

The new translation was completed in 406 and contains all the books of the OT that were circulating in Hebrew in his time, namely, the holy books accepted by the Jews, to which must be added the translation that he made from the Aramaic of the books of Judith and Tobit.

As can already be glimpsed on the basis of these brief biographical brushstrokes, Saint Jerome's work of translation, initiated by pontifical assignment, obliged him to face "textual" questions related to the Holy Scriptures which still today are the object of discussion, as was anticipated in the Introduction. Restricting ourselves to the OT, can we speak of a canonical

---

3. Cf. Jerome, *Letter* 125.12 (*Epistolary*, II, 597–98); Peña, "San Jerónimo," 285–300.
4. Cf. Jerome, *Letter* 84.3 (*Epistolary*, I, 889).
5. Jerome, *Letter* 106.2 (*Epistolary*, II, 152).

text? If so, which is it? In what language is that canonical text? Which passages does it include and which does it exclude? On what text should our liturgical translations be based? Can an ancient version come to be more important that the text on which it is based? Is it possible to speak of inspired translators?

All these are questions that Saint Jerome explicitly posed to himself as he proceeded with the translation of the various biblical books. Already in the prologue to his revision of the gospels he showed awareness of the criticisms and the resistance that his work would face, and this even though this was a pontifical assignment which was more than justified by the very numerous divergences among manuscripts:

> Pious labor, but dangerous presumption, that he should judge over others who himself should justly be judged by all, and that he should change the tongue of the old world and turn this, already hoary with age, back to earliest infancy! For who, whether learned or ignorant, when he has taken the volume in his hands and has seen that what he is reading differs from the saliva that he swallowed of old, will not raise his voice and cry that I am a man of sacrilege, I who dare to add, change or correct anything in the ancient books?[6]

What Jerome foreshadowed or prophesied was abundantly fulfilled, especially when he took the Hebrew text as a reference for the Latin translation of the OT. This decision gave rise to a heated polemic which, however, contributed to identifying with greater clarity the textual problems at stake. Indeed, a decision which today seems to us to be more than reasonable, such as the one to translate from the original text and not from another translation, entailed a series of aporias in its application to the OT, which had to come to light and which could only do so if each one of the opposing positions openly expounded its reasons.

THE REACTION OF AUGUSTINE TO JEROME'S *HEBRAICA VERITAS* PRINCIPLE

For a debate like this, a figure of the stature of Jerome was needed, not only with a sufficient knowledge of the Bible but with the courage necessary to confront the irascible monk of Bethlehem. This figure was Saint Augustine, bishop of Hippo, in North Africa. The epistolary correspondence that he

---

6. Jerome, *Pr. Ev.* (*Complete Works*, II, 509).

maintained with Saint Jerome, in the last years of the fourth century and the first of the fifth, represents a paradigmatic place to observe, in action, the terms of the textual problem to which reference has been made above.

The first letter that Augustine addressed to Jerome did not reach its destination. It is dated around the years 392–394. In it, the bishop of Hippo alluded to the new translations or revisions of the Greek which the Dalmatian doctor had made.[7] Even then Augustine expressed his unease at the implicit revision of the text of the LXX that was implied by translating into Latin the parts between asterisks which appeared in the fifth column of Origen, that is, the words from the Hebrew text that were not found in the Greek version. He was at least mollified by the fact that the reproduction of the Aristarchian symbols (obeli and asterisks) made it possible to recognize the authoritative work (LXX), by distinguishing it from the new additions, which were lacking in authority.[8]

Ten years later the correspondence was renewed. After Jerome asked Augustine for clarifications about a letter that was circulating around Rome, presumably addressed to him, the bishop of Hippo wrote a lengthy missive in which he incorporated copies of two letters that had not reached their destination. This was around the year 402–3 and the bishop of North Africa was already informed about the new translations from Hebrew undertaken by Jerome:

> In this letter I add that subsequently I learned that you have translated the book of Job from Hebrew, when we already had a translation of the same prophet, made by you from Greek into Latin . . .
>
> The truth is that I would prefer that you should translate the Greek canonical Scriptures which circulate under the name of the Seventy Interpreters. It would be truly lamentable, if your version begins to be read with frequency in many churches, that disagreement should arise between the Latin churches and the Greek ones, especially bearing in mind how easy it is to point the finger at the dissident by merely opening the Greek codices, that is, those in a very well known language. On the other hand, if anyone is puzzled by an unusual passage in the translation from the Hebrew, and claims to see in it a crime of falsification, it may perhaps never,

---

7. Cf. Jerome, *Letter* 56.2 (*Epistolary*, I, 537).

8. "With regard to translating into the Latin language the canonical Holy Scriptures, I would not wish for you to work on that, except it be in the same way that you have translated Job, showing, by means of appropriate symbols, the difference that there is between your translation and that of the Seventy, whose authority is exceedingly important" (Augustine, *Letter* 56.2 [*Epistolary*, I, 537]).

or almost never, be possible to go back to the Hebrew text with which the objection could be resolved. And even if that were to happen, who would tolerate having so many Greek and Latin authorities condemned? To this it must be added that if the Jews are consulted, they can respond in turn with a different translation, so that you would be the only one who could convince them. But who would serve as judge, if one could be found at all?[9]

The reason which Augustine adduces for advising against a translation from the Hebrew, namely, the danger of disagreement between the Latin churches and the Greek ones, is not merely theoretical. Below, he offers an example of something which happened when the new translation of Jerome began to be copied and transmitted:

> A certain bishop, our brother, had decreed that in the church which he governed your translation should be read. A passage of the prophet Jonah, translated by you in a way very different from that which had been engraved on the senses and in the memory of all, and the way it had been sung throughout the long succession of generations, brought about perplexity. Such a great tumult arose in the town, especially in the face of the protests and the ardor of the Greeks who considered the passage false, that the bishop—the city was Oea—found himself obliged to turn to the Jews to defend himself. I do not know whether from ignorance or malice, they responded that in the Hebrew codices the same appeared which was in the Greek and the Latin ones. What more was needed? The man, not wanting to find himself without a town, after a great conflict, found himself forced to correct his error. That is why I think that you too may have made a mistake sometime on some point.[10]

What is the heart of the problem stirred up by the new version? A modern reader, even moreso one who has had no training in translation, might feel lost in this discussion. Let me try to shed a little light. First of all, there are three languages involved: Hebrew, Greek, and Latin. The first, in the era of interest here, is spoken only by the Jews. Greek, on the other hand, is the language of the *ecumene*, the imperial language in which Christianity and its earliest documents were birthed, although since the third century it has been displaced by Latin in the Western part, to which Jerome and Augustine belong. Even so, in the education of erudite individuals who had Latin as their mother tongue, the study of Greek was normally included,

---

9. Augustine, *Letter* 104.34 (*Epistolary*, II, 141–42).
10. Augustine, *Letter* 104.5 (*Epistolary*, II, 143).

so that they could at least check the agreement between a Latin translation and its Greek original.

Likewise, there were three biblical "texts" that were dealt with in the discussions. On the one hand, the Hebrew text, which can provisionally be called "original," although only because of the fact that most of the books of the OT were originally written in Hebrew. This is a text to which access can only be gained through the manuscripts which the Jews possessed.[11] On the other hand, the Greek text of the Septuagint, translated from the Hebrew by the Jews of Alexandria between the end of the third century and the end of the second century B.C.E., was the text that was circulating among the Greek synagogues of the Mediterranean when Christianity expanded in the first and second centuries C.E., so that it constituted "the Scriptures" of the Greek-language Christians from the beginning. In the time in which Augustine and Jerome were exchanging letters, this version was known in slightly varying textual forms, as has been pointed out above, specifically the "recensions" of Hesychius, in Alexandria and Egypt, that of Lucian, in Antioch, and that of Origen, in Palestine.

Moreover, in clear polemic with the Christians, the Jews, discarding the version of the LXX, had produced two new Greek translations, very faithful to the Hebrew manuscripts that were being used by the Jews in the second century C.E.: those of Aquila and Symmachus, in addition to a third which should rather be considered a revision, that of Theodotion.[12] All three were available to the Christians through the Hexapla of Origen.

Finally, as a third biblical "text," in the Western part of the Roman Empire, from the second century C.E. on, there had spread a Latin translation

---

11. The Hebrew text of the first column of the Hexapla (which from the middle of the third century could be consulted in the Library of Origen in Caesarea) derives from manuscripts transmitted by the Jews.

12. The studies of Dominique Barthélemy (cf. Barthélemy, *Devanciers d'Aquila*) have revolutionized the image that we had of Theodotion as a Jew who did his revision at the end of the second century C.E. (information based on Epiphanius, *Mens. pond.* 17). Today it is generally thought, on the basis of manuscripts of the first century C.E. in which there is already evidence of a revision of the Greek text of the LXX, that Theodotion made his edition in the first half of this century (cf. Gentry, "Pre-Hexaplaric Translations," 226–27). In this way it could be understood why the Gospel of John (John 19:37) cites Zech 12:10 according to a version that is neither MT nor LXX but almost identical to Theodotion (cf. Bynum, *Fourth Gospel*; Menken, "Textual Form"). In Jerome's time, perhaps influenced by the order of the columns of the Hexapla, it was thought that Theodotion was a Jew who, like Aquila and Symmachus, and after them, was correcting the text of the LXX in polemic with its use by the Christians (cf. Jerome, *Letter* 112.19 [*Epistolary*, II, 307–8]).

done by Christians from the Greek version of the LXX. Together with the corresponding Latin translation of the NT, it constituted what is today called the *Vetus Latina*. Very soon, especially in the NT, this came to be known in quite variant forms which prevailed, respectively, in different places in the Empire (North Africa, the Italian peninsula, the Iberian peninsula, etc.), to the point of motivating the aforementioned request to Jerome, on the part of Pope Saint Damasus, for a revision.

Augustine, who wrote in Latin and read the Bible in the same language, was aware of the errors and deficiencies of the *Vetus Latina*, while at the same time showing himself to be knowledgeable of the textual plurality exhibited by the manuscripts of the Greek Bible which were circulating among the Christians. For this reason, recognizing the abilities of Jerome in the art of translation (and perhaps aware of the original pontifical mandate), he approved and encouraged the initiative of the monk of Bethlehem in doing a new Latin translation which reflected the original translation which we know as the Septuagint.

By this point, one can see as more than logical Augustine's concern about a single Latin text that does not differ from the one that is read in the Greek-language churches. A modern reader might conclude that the best thing would be to support Jerome's initiative: to turn to the Hebrew original and thus unify all the translations in other languages. However, what we consider to be the solution is the origin of the problem. This is how the bishop of Hippo lays it out in a letter to Jerome dated in the year 405:

> My reason for wanting your translation of the Seventy is . . . to see if it is possible for those who think that I am envious of your useful works can finally understand that the reason why I do not want your translation on the basis of the Hebrew to be read in the churches is in order not to diminish the authority of the Seventy and thus upset, with considerable scandal, and as if for love of novelty, the Christian people, whose ears and hearts are accustomed to hearing that translation, which, moreover, was approved by the apostles.[13]

Thus we come to the heart of the problem: Augustine considers that the Greek translation of the LXX has the authority of the apostles, for which reason it must serve as the starting point without any need for turning to the Hebrew, a language which, in any case, very few Christians could know. Jerome's new version contradicts this principle. In this way the

---

13. Augustine, *Letter* 116.35 (*Epistolary*, II, 352–53).

aforementioned textual problems come to light in a clear and orderly manner: Is it possible to speak of a canonical text of the OT? In what language is that text? On what text should our liturgical translations be based? Can an ancient version come to be superior to the text which it is translating?

CHAPTER 2

The Textual Differences between the Hebrew and the Greek Bibles

BEFORE PROCEEDING TO DESCRIBE in a detailed manner the principles that are in opposition in the polemic between Jerome and Augustine, and the reasons that support them, it is necessary to pause to study the essence of the problem, or to put it another way, the textual differences between the Hebrew manuscripts that were circulating in the fourth century C.E. among the Jews (which were essentially the same as those on which the new translations of Aquila and Symmachus were based) and the Greek text of the LXX with which the Christians of that same time were dealing. Only by becoming aware of these differences will it be possible to take seriously the discussion which was underway and to be in a position to assess their solutions, without downplaying a problem which has come down to our time and which requires breadth of perspective to be understood and, as appropriate, resolved.

This exposition, obviously, cannot be exhaustive. My purpose here is to present some paradigmatic cases which can aid in seeing the terms and the dimensions of the problem, that is, of the textual divergences between the Hebrew and Greek (LXX) texts of the OT.

THE BOOK OF JEREMIAH: TWO EDITIONS

I will begin with one of the clearest examples, albeit of a rather exceptional nature within the textual history of the OT. It is the book of Jeremiah. In the

Greek version of the LXX the text that is read is one-seventh shorter than the one found in the Hebrew manuscripts used by the Jews. This is rather strange since it is a translation, which tends to be a little longer than the original text (due to the translation techniques). In fact, in the case in question, the differences cannot be traced back to errors of the translator or the copyists. It is not a matter of words or lines that have been skipped, perhaps because of lapses in concentration. Sometimes whole sections are missing (such as MT 33:14–26 or 39:4–13, which are missing in the LXX). In other cases what is missing are the phrases that introduce a particular section (for example, Jer 2:1–2a and 27:1, which introduce oracles in the MT, are missing in the Greek version). But the differences are not only ones of content. In the LXX there is different organization of the material translated. The oracles against the nations, which in the Hebrew text close the book, in the LXX are placed in the middle, after chapter 25.[1]

In all likelihood this is a case of two different editions of the book of Jeremiah. The Greek version of the LXX seems to have translated a first Hebrew edition of the book of Jeremiah, which was shorter and had a different order of part of the material. Over time, as frequently happened in the history of the composition of the biblical books of the OT (and of the books of Antiquity in general) the book became known in a second edition which expanded it with new sections and finishing touches here and there, and moved the oracles against the nations to the final part of the book. This is the edition that was circulating in the temple in the time of Jesus and the one which Pharisaic rabbinism used and transmitted[2] down to the era of concern here. The exceptional thing about the history of this book is that the first Hebrew edition began to be copied and to circulate before undergoing the changes of the second edition. So much so that, in the period straddling the third and second centuries B.C.E., when the second edition was already circulating, the manuscript used to translate the book of Jeremiah into Greek, in Alexandria, was the one which contained the first edition.

The discovery of the Dead Sea manuscripts, beginning in 1947, has confirmed this theory. Until then, what I have called the "first edition" had

---

1. Cf. Tov, "Literary History."

2. The Judaism of the second century C.E. onward, which transmitted the Hebrew biblical text down to our day, can be properly called rabbinic Pharisaism or Pharisaic rabbinism, in the sense that the Pharisees, organized as teachers in the synagogues, are the only stream of Judaism which, together with the "messianic" or "Christian" Jews, survived the successive confrontations with the Romans.

not come down to us in Hebrew. Its existence could be deduced on the basis of the testimony of the Greek version. In the caves of Qumran there were found two fragments of the manuscript in Hebrew, 4QJr^b and 4QJr^d, which contain a text which differs in content and in the arrangement of material, compared to the Hebrew text known until then, and which bears great similarity to the Greek version of the LXX.

HEBREW TEXTUAL PLURALITY

Which edition of the Hebrew text of Jeremiah should we read today? Was Augustine right when he insisted that when he was reading the LXX, he was reading the most "original" edition, or will we agree with Jerome when he claimed to offer the "definitive" edition of the book? This example helps us to understand that, beyond the book of Jeremiah, the relationship between the Hebrew text which the Jews used and the Greek version of the LXX was not always, by any means, the relationship between an original text and its translation. Properly speaking, the Hebrew text which Jerome was translating was what is called a Proto-Masoretic text, that is, the consonantal, unvocalized text which was circulating in Palestine at least in the second century C.E. and which the Jews transmitted until it was vocalized, accented, and supplied with masora by the Masoretes (Jewish scribes) starting in the seventh century C.E., constituting the Masoretic Text (MT) that is currently known.

Today it is known that this was not the only Hebrew text type derived from the hypothetical original which came from the hands of the sacred authors. The Greek version of the LXX testifies, in many points, to a different Hebrew text type. In most cases the differences go back to Hebrew variants in relation to the Proto-Masoretic text which, depending on the case, can be judged original or secondary. In other cases it is a matter of different "editions" of the Hebrew text, as happens in Jeremiah. A third Hebrew text type is the one found in the Samaritan Pentateuch, the Hebrew text of the five books of the Law transmitted by the community of the Samaritans (who only recognized as canonical the books of the Pentateuch), separated from Jerusalem, and which still survives in the city of Nablus (Shechem) and other small, scattered communities. Setting aside the additions of a "sectarian" kind, the Samaritan Pentateuch preserves Hebrew variants which could be original and which, on occasion, agree with the Hebrew *Vorlage* of the LXX (that is, the Hebrew text which underlies the

The Textual Differences between the Hebrew and the Greek Bibles

Greek translation) against the Proto-Masoretic text (or MT if the variants which have to do with vocalization are included).

Although it is certainly exceptional, the case of Jeremiah is not the only example of a different edition of the Hebrew text. The Greek text (LXX) of Ezekiel is 4 or 5 percent shorter than the MT,[3] while that of Joshua contains shorter sections and other longer ones, always in relation to the MT.[4] In both cases there are small parts whose arrangement within the book varies from one edition to another. In other books, differences between the Hebrew and Greek texts are found in particular chapters which might be traced back to different Hebrew editions. This is the case in 1 Sam 2:1–10 (Song of Hannah), 1 Samuel 16–18, and Nehemiah 11:25–35.[5] What should be done in these cases? Which edition should be privileged? Which contender should be considered the right one?

JOB, OR WHEN THE TRANSLATOR DOES NOT UNDERSTAND

The case of the book of Job deserves separate comment. The original Greek translation of the LXX is one-sixth shorter than the MT (some 390 fewer verses). This is not, however, a case of a different Hebrew edition at the origin of the translation, as happened with Jeremiah. Most authors agree that in this case, the translator of the LXX, finding himself looking at probably the most complicated Hebrew text in the whole Bible, made numerous omissions of verses which he did not understand or which injured his theological sensibilities, or he simply paraphrased them.[6]

3. Cf. Tov, "Large-Scale Differences," 126. The *Chester Beatty* papyrus 967 contains a Greek text of Ezekiel in which two short sections and one long one are missing in relation to the LXX, in addition to showing a different order in some sections in relation to the MT and LXX. Some authors think that this is the original form of the LXX, which was later completed on the basis of the Hebrew (Johnson et al., *Ezekiel*; Ziegler, "Chester Beatty"). John Lust thinks that this Greek original version is based on a first Hebrew edition prior to the one reflected in the MT (Lust, "Textual Criticism," 28–31).

4. Cf. Tov, "Large-Scale Differences," 127. On the basis of a study of the first twelve chapters of the book of Joshua, Kristin de Troyer concludes that "underlying the Old Greek text, there was a Hebrew text, which is *slightly different and slightly elder* than the Hebrew Masoretic Text. In my opinion, the Hebrew Masoretic Text is the ultimate text of the book of Joshua and the Hebrew *Vorlage* underlying the Old Greek text is the penultimate one!" (Troyer, *Joshua*, 170).

5. Cf. Tov, "Large-Scale Differences," 129–30.

6. According to Maria Gorea, the abbreviated translations and the omissions may

Hebraica veritas versus Septuaginta auctoritatem

This short text has not survived in Greek manuscripts. It is known only through the testimony of the Sahidic Coptic version and the original *Vetus Latina*, cited by the Latin Fathers Cyprian (mid-third century C.E.) and Lucifer of Cagliari (mid-fourth century C.E.)[7] and Jerome himself.[8] The Greek text found in the great codices that have come down to us (*Sinaiticus, Vaticanus, Alexandrinus,* and *Ephraemi Syri Rescriptus*), which represent the basis of the critical editions of the LXX, is a "mixed" text which incorporates numerous verses taken from the version of Theodotion to fill in the "holes" which the original translator left. Even so, it is somewhat shorter than the Hebrew which the MT represents. It is the text which is known as "ecclesiastical."

A third step is found in the Hexaplaric manuscripts which attest to the systematic and complete work of Origen, who produced a Greek text of the same length as the Hebrew, taking from Theodotion all that was missing (in relation to the Hebrew) in the early Greek translation. This is the Greek text which Jerome translated into Latin (before his translation from the

---

be explained because the Greek translator shows a theological sensibility quite different from the one at the origin of the book of Job. Perhaps he considered some passages disrespectful, or others unnecessary because they delay the denouement. In fact, at the beginning the omissions are not numerous. They increase as the work goes along, as if showing the impatience of the translator and his decision to shape the exaggerated features of the character of Job. It is even possible, in some translations, to catch a certain sympathy toward the friends of Job and their speeches. As a consequence of the omissions, the translator has syntactical problems with linking together what he is translating. It is as if the resulting syntax ignored the omitted text. Moreover, the difficulty of the Hebrew language of this book (perhaps the most complicated book in the OT from the philological point of view) may have motivated a number of omissions. The translator may have eliminated passages that were obscure, ambiguous or difficult to interpret (Cf. Gorea, *Job repensé*, 223–28). Cf. Cox, "Job." The contrary hypothesis, that is, that the short Greek text reflects a shorter first Hebrew edition, was first supported by Edwin Hatch in 1889 (Hatch, *Biblical Greek*). In the second half of the twentieth century, the author who most strongly supported the precedence of the short Greek text was Harry M. Orlinsky, in a series of articles published in the journal *Hebrew Union College Annual* (*HUCA*) between 1957 and 1965. He was refuted by Cox, "Hebrew Parent Text."

7. Cf. Bogaert, "Job"; Feder, "Job."

8. "But among the Latins, before the translation which we published a short time ago with asterisks and obeli, almost seven hundred or eight hundred verses are missing, such that the book, cut down and tattered, and also corroded, presents its ugly appearance to the readers" (Jerome, *Pr. Job heb.* [*Complete Works*, II, 487]). The "seven hundred or eight hundred verses" are in fact "hemistichs" or lines, within the structure of parallelism of Hebrew poetry, so they are equivalent to a total of 350 or 375 verses, which coincides with the calculations that are made today about the difference in length between the version of the LXX and MT in Job.

The Textual Differences between the Hebrew and the Greek Bibles

Hebrew), preserving the Aristarchian symbols (obeli and asterisks). This first Latin translation of Jerome was approved and cited by Augustine.[9]

Returning to the polemic between these two holy doctors, should our modern versions be based on a short text which was the result of a translator's lack of skill, turn to the mixed text present in the manuscripts of the LXX, or translate from the difficult but complete original Hebrew text?

THE CURIOUS HISTORY OF THE GREEK DANIEL

Another biblical book that has a curious textual history, which is of interest in the present discussion, is that of Daniel. The original translation of the LXX is only preserved in two Greek manuscripts: *Codex Chisianus* (Rahlfs 88) and the very important *Chester Beatty* papyrus (Rahlfs 967, dated around the second–third centuries C.E.). It is indirectly attested, moreover, by the Syro-Hexapla version.[10] This Greek text presents notable differences with respect to the MT, especially in Dan 4–6, to the point that some consider it probable that the translator had before him a different edition of the Hebrew-Aramaic text.[11] Specifically, in the aforementioned Greek papyrus 967, chapters 7–8 appear after Dan 4.[12]

Starting in the third century C.E., for some unknown reason, the original translation was rejected and replaced, in ecclesiastical use, by the version of Theodotion, who follows the Hebrew and Aramaic text known to us.[13] This replacement was so radical that it affected the whole manuscript transmission of the Septuagint (excepting the *Codex Chisianus*), so that the version of Theodotion became the ecclesiastical text of Daniel. The *Vetus*

---

9. Cf. Augustine, *Letter* 56.2 (*Epistolary*, I, 537).

10. Amara, "Daniel," 542.

11. Cf. Amara, "Daniel. Septuagint"; Segal, "Daniel 5"; Segal, "Old Greek Version"; Kooij, "Compositions and Editions."

12. The text of the *Codex Chisianus* follows the order of the chapters of the MT and Theodotion. It probably underwent the influence of the arrangement of the latter, which wound up being the ecclesiastical order.

13. "The book of the prophet Daniel according to the Seventy Interpreters is not read by the churches of the Lord and Savior, which make use of the edition of Theodotion, and why this has happened, I know not. For if it was because their language is Chaldean and it disagrees with our language in some properties and the Seventy Interpreters refused to preserve the same lines in the translation, or if the book was published under the name of them by I know not whom else, one not very well versed in the Chaldean language, or if there was another cause, this only can I affirm: that it disagrees much with the truth and that it is repudiated by a just judgment" (Jerome, *Pr. Dan.* [*Complete Works*, II, 503–5]).

Latina was also affected by this process, so that the manuscripts which have come down to us follow the text of Theodotion and the original Latin translation is only preserved, in a very fragmentary way, in the citations of Tertullian and Cyprian.[14]

Again the question arises: in the case of Daniel, on which text should our modern translations be based? On the ecclesiastical text which is not the original text of the LXX? On the Hebrew text that does not have the canonical "additions" in Greek? On the fragmentary testimony of Greek papyrus 967? On a partial Latin reconstruction on the basis of the citations of Tertullian and Cyprian?

Since I have mentioned the Greek additions in Daniel, I should take the opportunity to present other divergences that do not lead back to different Hebrew text types at the origin of the translation, but to parts or sections of books that were incorporated into the Greek version of the LXX in Alexandria once they were translated into Greek. In this sense they are called "additions." They are the sections preserved only in the Greek of Daniel (Dan 3:24–90; 13: Susanna; Dan 14: Bel and the Dragon) and of Esther (Est 10:4—16:24, according to the arrangement of the Vulgate).[15]

THE SPECIAL PROBLEMS OF THE DEUTEROCANONICAL BOOKS

Another of the notable differences between the Greek version of the LXX used by the Christians and the Hebrew text used by the Jews in the time of Saint Jerome was the number of books considered holy or canonical. The books of Tobit and Judith (which Jerome knew and translated from the Aramaic),[16] those of Sirach, 1 Maccabees, Baruch, and the Letter of Jeremiah (the original of which was in Hebrew), and those of Wisdom and 2 Maccabees (originally written in Greek) were rejected as Scripture by Pharisaic rabbinism starting in the second century C.E. and accepted by the Christians who found them translated into Greek among the books that

14. Cf. Cañas Reíllo, "Daniel."

15. The division into chapters and verses is based on the Vulgate. Saint Jerome grouped together in the final part of the book, as an appendix, all the Greek additions that were found scattered throughout the book in the version of the LXX. Our modern translations introduce each Greek "addition" in the proper place, following the arrangement of the Greek version of Esther.

16. Cf. Jerome, *Pr. Tob.* (*Complete Works*, II, 481) and *Pr. Jud.* (*Complete Works*, II, 481–83).

were read in the Greek synagogues. Precisely because of this, the Hebrew and Aramaic textual transmission of these books ceased, to the point that only copies in Greek have been preserved.[17]

In the case of these books, which are known as deuterocanonical, as in that of the Greek fragments of Daniel and Esther, the first question that is asked is whether they should be translated in order to be used in the liturgy. The answer to this question is simpler than the previous ones, since they are texts which were recognized dogmatically as canonical in the Council of Trent. When the question was asked at the end of the fourth century its answer was somewhat more complex, to the point that Jerome considered them to be among the apocryphal books.[18]

Once an affirmative reply has been given, a second question arises which the most recent modern translations have had to face: Should the book of Sirach be translated from the Greek or from the recently discovered incomplete Hebrew text? The problems do not end there. In the event that the translation is done from the Greek, from which of the two surviving editions should it be done? Although the textual problem of this book is very complicated, it seems that the Hebrew original was known in two different editions, and they are the basis for the two Greek editions known to us, the second of which is the product of the revision of Origen and Lucian. The Latin translation (*Vetus*) does not follow either of the two Greek editions but rather seems to attest to a Greek *Vorlage* halfway between the two. The Syriac Peshitta version, for its part, translates from the Hebrew and seems to have had before it both editions in the original language.[19]

The same question could be asked with regard to the book of Tobit. Until the middle of the nineteenth century, the whole manuscript tradition of the LXX presented a "short" version of the book. The discovery of the *Codex Sinaiticus* (the oldest complete codex of the Greek Bible together with the *Vaticanus*, both from the fourth century C.E.) in 1859 brought to light a more expansive version, laden with Semitisms, and the Qumran discoveries yielded fragments in Aramaic (almost half the book) and in

---

17. In the case of Sirach, first in the Cairo Geniza, at the end of the nineteenth century, and subsequently among the manuscripts of the Dead Sea caves (Qumran and Masada), starting in 1947, some three-fourths of the original Hebrew text has come to light. Also in the Dead Sea caves, four copies with fragments in Aramaic and one with fragments in Hebrew of the book of Tobit have been found.

18. Cf. Jerome, *Pr. Galeatus* (*Complete Works*, II, 455–61).

19. For a study of the complex textual question of Sirach, cf. Wright, "Ben Sira"; Morla, *Manuscritos hebreos de Ben Sira*; Beentjes, *Book of Ben Sira*.

Hebrew (a very small portion). In fact, some Greek manuscripts attest to a third version which represents a kind of compromise between the two main ones. Bearing in mind that the relationships between the Greek versions and the Aramaic and Hebrew fragments has not been clarified, should translations be made from the longer Greek version, which is the basis for the *Vetus Latina* and which for many represents the original Greek version, or should they be made from the short Greek version, which some argue is the original? Bearing in mind that the Vulgate includes the Latin translation which Jerome made from the Aramaic, which coincides with the short version, should translations be made from this Latin version? Or should they perhaps be made from the Aramaic fragments which have been preserved, bearing in mind that they do not agree with the Aramaic text that Jerome had before him?[20]

AND AN ENDLESS NUMBER OF DIFFERENCES IN DETAILS . . .

By way of bringing to a close this long series of divergences between the Greek and Hebrew texts in dispute, I should allude to the interminable list of differences which do not affect longer or shorter sections (which may or may not go back to different Hebrew editions in their origin) but individuals words or expressions. As is well known from the paradigmatic example of Isa 7:14 (LXX: παρθένος, *virgin*; MT: עלמה, *young damsel*), many of these differences constituted the material over which Jews and Christians contended, especially during the second and third centuries C.E. Bearing in mind that Jerome was attempting to translate *ex novo* from the Hebrew, these divergences in details again came to the center of the discussion, this time among Christians. Since the contenders themselves, Jerome and Augustine, brought them up, I will illustrate them below, in connection with the description of the polemic.

---

20. On the textual problem of Tobit, cf. Littman, "Textual History of Tobit." Toloni, *Tobia*.

The Textual Differences between the Hebrew and the Greek Bibles

THE HEXAPLA OF ORIGEN AS A KEY INSTRUMENT FOR IDENTIFYING THE DIVERGENCES

Throughout this exposition I have had occasion to allude to the work of Origen known as the Hexapla. Precisely because of the role that this great enterprise, carried out in the mid-third century C.E., had in the understanding of the relationship between the Hebrew text and the Greek text of the LXX in the time in which Jerome and Augustine were arguing, it is necessary to pause for another moment before taking on the task I have set for myself, namely, to describe in detail the principles that are in conflict in the polemic in question.

Origen created a work in which he arranged his material in six columns (thus the Greek *Hexapla*) with the intention of comparing the biblical text in Hebrew which was circulating in his time with the different Greek versions known at that moment, especially the Septuagint, used by the Christians.[21] In the first column he displayed the Hebrew text in Hebrew characters (at that time unvocalized). In the second he set out a Greek transliteration of the Hebrew text as it should sound when read, which implied a vocalization that did not appear in the first column. The third, fourth and sixth columns displayed, respectively, the Greek translations of Aquila, Symmachus, and Theodotion. Finally, the fifth column presented the ecclesiastical text of the LXX, although in a curious critical edition done with the help of the Aristarchian symbols, which were usual in the work of textual criticism of the classical Alexandrian school.[22]

This fifth column was the heart of the Hexapla, because it made it possible to identify simply and effectively the divergences between the ecclesiastical text and the one used by the Jews. For this purpose Origen marked, with an obelus at the beginning and a metobelus at the end, those parts of the LXX that were not found in the Hebrew manuscripts. On the other hand, he added, marking it with an asterisk at the beginning and a metobelus at the end, a Greek translation of what was read in Hebrew and

---

21. About the motives that pushed Origen to produce a work of this caliber, cf. Law, "Origen's Parallel Bible"; Sgherri, "valutazione origeniana"; Barthélemy, "Origène et le texte."

22. Aristarchus of Samothrace (ca. 217–145 B.C.E.), grammarian, director of the Library of Alexandria in the mid-second century. He is known as the critical editor of the works attributed to Homer, the Iliad and the Odyssey. In order to make critical editions which would separate the original readings from the later interpolations, he created the symbols which we know as Aristarchian. Cf. Kirk, "Aristarchus and the Scholia."

did not appear in the LXX. The material marked with an asterisk was not a translation *ex novo* made from the Hebrew by the Alexandrian. According to his own testimony, those parts were incorporated "from the other versions which agreed with the Hebrew,"[23] namely, Aquila, Symmachus, or Theodotion. Jerome, who was able to consult the Hexapla in Caesarea, states that that material came from Theodotion.[24]

Unfortunately, this work has not come down to us.[25] In fact, many doubt that it was ever copied in its entirety, that is, with its six columns (in some books more than six). Indeed, who would have the ability to copy the first Hebrew column? What utility would Christians find in those signs which they did not know how to read? It is more likely that the book would have circulated as a Tetrapla,[26] that is, displaying the four Greek columns in parallel.

What is certain is that the fifth column became a real "best seller" and was copied and transmitted with its Aristarchian symbols for a long time.[27] In a way, it represented a "complete" text, with the virtue that it distinguished the provenance of the material and turned out to be a great help not only for discussion with the Jews but also for the production of exegetical commentaries. The counterbalance of this, though, was that the independent transmission of this fifth column introduced great confusion into the manuscript tradition of the LXX, since the Aristarchian symbols

---

23. ἵνα δῆλον ᾖ ὅτι μὴ κείμενα παρὰ τοῖς Ἑβδομήκοντα ἐκ τῶν λοιπῶν ἐκδόσεων συμφώνως τῷ Ἑβραϊκῷ προσεθήκαμεν (Origen, *Comm. Matt.* 15.14).

24. Cf. *Letter* 112.19 (*Epistolary*, II, 308).

25. A notable exception are the fragments of Psalms that have been found both in the Biblioteca Ambrosiana (Rahlfs 1098) and in the Cairo Geniza (Rahlfs 2005), both of which are in palimpsests, which preserve the arrangement in columns of the original work (Mercati, *Psalterii Hexapli reliquiae*; Taylor, *Genizah Palimpsest*).

26. As some sources have described it (Eusebius, *Hist. eccl.* 6.16 and the colophons of the Syro-Hexapla), the work of Origen was transmitted in the form of a Tetrapla, excluding the first two columns. On the one hand, few Christian copyists would have been able to copy the Hebrew of the first column, while on the other hand, few would have been interested in the Greek transcription of the Hebrew text located in the second column. Now Tetrapla does not necessarily mean a manuscript in four columns; it can mean material which preserves the information of the last four columns, in the image of what is seen in the Syro-Hexapla and in the Greek manuscript *Barber.* gr. 549 (Rahlfs 86): the text of the fifth column in the center and in the margins notes about the variant readings of Aquila, Symmachus, and Theodotion. Cf. Jenkins, "Hexaplaric Marginalia"; Jenkins, "Colophons of the Syrohexapla."

27. Testimony of this are the manuscripts Rahlfs 88 (*Codex Chisianus*) and Q (*Codex Marchalianus*).

The Textual Differences between the Hebrew and the Greek Bibles

were not always copied attentively.[28] Material that had never been part of the LXX (marked with asterisks) came to form part of this version in some manuscripts, precisely because of this type of copyist's error. On the other hand, some copyists, accustomed to the value of the obeli in the textual criticism of the classical works, that is, to mark passages that were considered to be non-original glosses, thought that they would be faithful to Origen's intention by eliminating those parts. Over time, the Origenian recension of the LXX, at least in some manuscripts, wound up being a calque from the Hebrew text, precisely what Origen wanted to avoid.[29]

Although I have spent some time on the description of the Hexapla, this is because this work introduced factors decisive to the understanding of the problem of interest here. The decisions that Jerome made with regard to Bible translation, and the content of the discussions that he had about it, specifically with Augustine, would not have been possible throughout the second century C.E. because of the simple fact that the textual information (in its Greek and Hebrew tradition) was scarce and insufficient. Nor would it have been possible at the end of the second century or the beginning of the third century, when the three new Greek translations or revisions of Aquila, Symmachus, and Theodotion were already known;[30] the synoptic work of Origen was necessary in order to *weigh* the data seriously with regard to the relationship between the Hebrew text and its Greek versions.

When Jerome settled in Bethlehem, in the year 386, he found himself three days by road (some one hundred km) from Caesarea, the place where Origen carried out his great work and where it was preserved at that time. Jerome himself reports that he was able to consult the Hexapla on various occasions, as is attested by the use he made of its columns in his exegetical works.[31] Moreover, in the first five years of his stay in Bethlehem he

---

28. "Origène avait conçu les hexaples comme une ample collection d'informations. Mais des glossateurs et correcteurs s'en servirent sans discernement pour retoucher le texte vulgaire de la Septante, alors qu'Origène avait donné de celle-ci une édition critique où il la traitait d'une manière autrement respectueuse. A part quelques papyri fragmentaires, il n'est pas un seul des manuscrits grecs de la Septante dont nous puissions certifier que les hexaples n'ont pas déteint sur lui de quelque manière" (Barthélemy, "Origène et le texte," 247).

29. Barthélemy, "Origène et le texte," 253.

30. Even Irenaeus alludes to the versions of Theodotion and Aquila in a discussion about Isa 7:14 (cf. Irenaeus, *Haer.* III, 21.1). Before Irenaeus, Justin seems to allude to the new versions, although he does not name them (cf. Justin, *Dial.* 71.1).

31. It is paradigmatic, in this sense, the use which Jerome makes of the readings of Aquila, Symmachus and Theodotion, as well as the Hebrew vocalization (which he could

translated a good number of biblical books from the Greek version of the fifth column into Latin, for which reason he became familiarized in great detail with the differences between the Hebrew text and the "ecclesiastical" version. We can imagine the effect that this daily, systematic work produced on the doctor from Stridon, especially when he realized the richness contained in those parts which were not attested in the LXX and which had been transmitted only in Hebrew manuscripts (marked with asterisks in the fifth column). Among them are found some passages of the OT cited in the NT which are not reflected in the ecclesiastical Greek version.

The very work of translation into Latin directly from Hebrew, undertaken starting in 390, benefitted from the Greek testimonies of Aquila, Symmachus, and Theodotion, preserved in the Hexapla, which, after all, had been translated from a Hebrew text very similar to the one that Jerome must have had in his hands. Although there is debate about the use which Jerome could have made of these late Greek versions,[32] just as there is debate about his very knowledge of Hebrew,[33] there is no doubt that the Latin translations contained in the Vulgate would not have been the same without an instrument like the one offered to him by the Hexapla.

Finally, the transliteration of the Hebrew into Greek, contained in the second column which he could consult in Caesarea, provided Jerome with the possibility of correctly interpreting the consonantal text he was gazing at in his Hebrew manuscripts. To translate from unvocalized Hebrew must not have been an easy task for a man like Saint Jerome, who was not accustomed from childhood to listening to or chanting the biblical text in its original language. He lacked a tradition of Jewish reading, which is what he could find both in the second column of the Hexapla, and in the counsel of rabbi Baranina, as the monk of Bethlehem himself confesses.[34] Actually, both traditions, in all likelihood, would have agreed, since they belonged to the same geographical area and were separated by somewhat more than a century.[35]

---

not find in the manuscripts of the Jews but in the second column of the Hexapla), in Letter 106, addressed to Sunnia and Fretela, which clarified corrupted passages in the manuscripts of the Psalter (Cf. *Letter* 106.4, 7, 9, 19, 28, 35, 41, 46, 50, 51, 63, 65, 68, 78 [*Epistolary*, II, 149–96]).

32. Cf. Gentry, "Role of the 'Three'"; Vaccari, "Esaple ed esaplare."
33. Cf. Newman, "Jerome's Hebrew Competence."
34. Cf. *Letter* 84.3 (*Epistolary*, I, 889).
35. The Greek transliteration of the Hebrew that is found in Origen's second column would have to be based on a Jewish reading tradition. G. Mercati, speaking about the

The Textual Differences between the Hebrew and the Greek Bibles

Augustine, for his part, never consulted the Hexapla, nor would it have been especially helpful to him, since he did not know Hebrew and his control of Greek, by his own confession, was not very fluent.[36] Nevertheless, the perception of the differences between the Hebrew biblical text and the Greek ecclesiastical text (which was the source of the Latin version that the bishop of Hippo used) had been made concrete and verifiable in his time through the copies of the fifth column (with its Aristarchian symbols) and, above all, through the Latin translations of some biblical books which Jerome made from that same fifth column.

Augustine, in fact, appreciated Jerome's work which, by preserving the Aristarchian symbols, allowed those who only knew the Latin language to familiarize themselves with the differences between the Hebrew Bible and the Christian OT. His esteem for Jerome's early works comes out precisely when Jerome abandons them and begins to translate directly from the Hebrew:

> I subsequently learned that you have translated the book of Job from the Hebrew, when we already had a translation of the same prophet, made by you from Greek into Latin, in which you indicated with asterisks what is found in the Hebrew and is lacking in the Greek, and with obeli what is found in the Greek and is lacking in the Hebrew.[37]

It was then that Augustine resorted to an argument that would not have been as immediate to him without the work of Origen (mediated by Jerome):

> In addition, in the later translation, made on the basis of the Hebrew, the same fidelity in the words is not seen. This disconcerts not a little anyone who thinks about why in the first the asterisks are placed with such scrupulous exactness to indicate even the most minimal parts of the sentence that are lacking in the Greek codices and were found in those in Hebrew, and why, on the other hand, in the second, which is made directly from the Hebrew, less

---

second column, states that "non vi possono essere direttamente rappresentate se non la vocalizzazione e la pronuncia dell'ebraico, quali usavano in sinagoghe e scuole ebraiche palestinensi del secolo III d.C." (Mercati, "colonna II dell'Esaplo," 210). With regard to the purpose of the second column, cf. Norton, "First Two Columns."

36. Augustine, *C. litt. Petil.* II, 38, 91. Cf. Marrou, *Saint Augustin*, 27–46; Marrou, *Retractatio*, 631–37.

37. Augustine, *Letter* 104.3 (*Epistolary*, II, 141).

diligence has been exercised to have those same symbols appear in their corresponding places.³⁸

In Jerome's first translation, made from the fifth column of the Hexapla, Augustine could become aware of the Hebrew parts that were lacking in the Greek manuscripts. But in addition, very specific notice was given of that which the Hebrew codices did not attest but which the Church had nonetheless been reading for more than three centuries. Therefore, when Jerome decided to abandon the Greek ecclesiastical version and translate solely from what he considered to be the original Hebrew text, Augustine reproached him for not making visible, with the same Aristarchian symbols, what the reader was missing in the age-old Christian reading contained in the LXX.

---

38. Augustine, *Letter* 104.3 (*Epistolary*, II, 141–42).

CHAPTER 3

The *Hebraica Veritas*
Lights

Now I AM IN a position to describe in detail the principles that are in conflict in this polemic and the reasons that support them. This, in turn, will allow us to face, in an informed manner, the question which has come down to our days and is pressing with regard to modern translations: Is it possible to speak of a canonical text of the OT?

In a very synthetic way, the two principles in competition could be formulated as *hebraica veritas versus Septuaginta auctoritatem*, supported respectively by Jerome and Augustine. In the view of the monk of Bethlehem, it would be necessary to translate from the Hebrew texts in which the *truth* was originally expressed, while in the view of Augustine, the Church could not be separated from the Greek text which had the authority of the apostles, who used it in the composition of the NT.[1]

In this and the next three chapters we will carefully study the two principles, so that we can understand the truth which they (fairly) claim to support (the "lights" of each principle: chapters 3 and 5) and so that, in turn, we can identify their weaknesses or, to put it another way, what they

---

1. "Devant un problème comme celui-ci, la lecture de la Bible, lecture officielle dans l'assemblée chrétienne, il [Augustin] avait le sentiment que 'l'autorité' avait à intervenir, en tenant compte de considérations qui lui sont propres. Parmi celles-ci, l'usage des églises, une coutume qui remonterait aux Apôtres. C'est tout cet ensemble qui réclamait l'attention. Aux yeux de Jérôme, à l'inverse, 'la vérité' devait avoir le pas dans cette affaire ; il l'appelait l'*hebraica veritas*. L'hébreu était premier, seul texte 'valable' selon lui" (Jouassard, "Réflexions," 99).

forget (and it is not fair to forget) (the "shadows" of each principle: chapters 4 and 6).

The polemic which I now present touches not only on questions of "text" but also on questions of canon. In fact, the principle of the *hebraica veritas* led Jerome to consider apocryphal those books which had not been received in Hebrew and were not in the canon of the Jews.[2] In my description of the principles in play I will take up solely the questions that touch on the text from which to start, and only farther on will I return to the canonical problem.

THE VALUE OF THE *HEBRAICA VERITAS* PRINCIPLE

The expression *hebraica veritas* is used by Jerome himself to refer to the divine truth as it has been expressed in the Scriptures, originally in Hebrew. In his prologue to the divine books translated by himself from Hebrew into Latin, known as the *Galeatus* prologue, he uses the aforementioned expression as the ultimate criterion of his translation from which he does not want to depart:

> Read, therefore, first my *Samuel* and *Malakim*; mine, I say, mine, because all that which, by translating it often and amending it with diligence we learn and retain, is our own. And when you shall have understood that which you previously did not know, consider me a translator if you are grateful, or a paraphraser, if ungrateful; although I am not at all aware of having changed any of the Hebraic truth (*de Hebraica veritate*).[3]

What are the reasons why Jerome arrives at this principle, which is decisive for his work of translation starting in 390? The prologues to the different books which he translated from Hebrew into Latin (in a span of some sixteen years) are a privileged place to discover the reasons which led the monk of Bethlehem to turn to the *hebraica veritas* contained in the manuscripts transmitted by the Jews. Below I will present these reasons in an orderly fashion, with all that is valid about them, and then point out the weaknesses in their argumentation.

---

2. In his *Galeatus prologue*, Jerome states: "This prologue . . . can be proper for all the books which we have translated from Hebrew into Latin, in order that we can know that any work which is outside of them must be placed among the apocryphal books" (*Complete Works*, II, 459).

3. Jerome, *Pr. Galeatus* (*Complete Works*, II, 461).

Bearing in mind the different places in which Jerome argues for his new principle, it is possible to identify three reasons which support it.

IN VIEW OF THE TEXTUAL CONFUSION OF THE LXX, LET US RETURN TO THE HEBREW ORIGINAL

The book of Chronicles is one of the few for which the prologues have been preserved which Jerome wrote to both the translation from the Greek and the translation from the Hebrew. A comparison of the two prologues provides extremely valuable material for identifying the reasons for the transition, which took place in the monk of Bethlehem, from the *Septuaginta auctoritas* to the *hebraica veritas*.

In the prologue to the first translation of the book of Chronicles, the doctor from Stridon acknowledges the confusion surrounding the names which is found in both the Greek manuscripts and the Latin ones. He believes that in those manuscripts "barbarian and Sarmatian" names have been added. The fault, however,

> should not be attributed to the Seventy Interpreters, who, aided by the Holy Spirit, translated the names which had been authentic, but rather the fault lies with the copyists, who incorrectly copied what was incorrect and often, taking syllables out of the middle, group three names into a single word or, on the other hand, a single name, because of its length, they divide into two or three words.[4]

At that time, prior to 390, Jerome was supporting the LXX as a starting point which had the help of the Holy Spirit and the authority of tradition. His labor as a translator, however, led him to confirm the disconcerting plurality of the Greek manuscripts, which is reflected in the Latin ones. The task of the doctor of Bethlehem was that of recovering the "original" form of the LXX, blurred at that time by the activity of the copyists. The Hexapla of Origen played a fundamental role in this task, and most specifically the fifth column in which the Alexandrian made a double effort: one of purification, by presenting a text of the LXX which was free of the additions and errors of copyists, and one of comparison, by indicating the *pluses* and *minuses* in relation to the Hebrew text.

---

4. Jerome, *Pr. Par. gr.* (*Complete Works*, II, 471).

Hebraica veritas versus Septuaginta auctoritatem

Although Jerome respected the authority of the LXX, in this prologue a principle is introduced which over time will lead him to forcefully affirm the *hebraica veritas*. To bring order to the textual confusion of the LXX, it seemed natural and practically obvious to the Dalmatian to turn to the Hebrew manuscripts in the possession of the Jews. This was an enterprise which Origen began and which Jerome transferred to the Latin translations. In the same prologue to the Latin translation of Chronicles from the Greek, the monk of Bethlehem is already showing signs of this pull toward the Hebrew form as an arbiter:

> If anyone wants to reprehend anything in this version, let him ask the Hebrews, let him turn to their sensible competence, let him see the order and composition of the discourse and then, if he can, let him censure our work. Therefore, wherever in this book you see asterisks shining, that is, stars, know that here something has been added, brought in from the Hebrew, which is not found in our Latin codices; but where an obelus, that is, a crosswise downstroke, has been placed, there is indicated something which the *Seventy Interpreters* have added, whether for the sake of elegance or also by virtue of the authority of the Holy Spirit, even though it is not read in the Hebrew scrolls.[5]

Jerome takes it for granted that what is not attested in the Hebrew manuscripts at his disposal has been *added* by the Seventy Interpreters, although he still defends these additions as necessary "for the sake of elegance" or as being wanted by the Holy Spirit.

In the prologue to the second translation of the book of Chronicles, this time from the Hebrew, Jerome turns back to the problem of the textual variety of the manuscripts of the LXX (he alludes to the three "recensions" of the text which have come down to him: that of Hesychius, that of Lucian and that of Origen). On this occasion, however, he takes a step forward by presenting an alternative to bring order to the confusion,

> or rather to judge, among the many recensions, which is the true one or also to establish upon the old work a new work.[6]

If in his first version from the Greek he took the first path, the monk of Bethlehem sees that the time has come to take the second, making a "new work" from the "old work," which is, obviously, the one which is preserved

---

5. Jerome, *Pr. Par. gr.* (*Complete Works*, II, 473).
6. Jerome, *Pr. Par. heb.* (*Complete Works*, II, 473).

in the Hebrew manuscripts. It is these latter manuscripts which will judge the value of his work and to which he refers when confronting criticisms:

> Why are my Latin brethren not going to accept me, who upon the ancient virgin version have created another new one and in such a way that I can prove the goodness of my labor with the text of the Hebrews?[7]

The transition has culminated: the Hebrew text is considered the "ancient virgin version" (*inviolata editione veteri*), free of corruption and the point of reference to clarify any doubt about the versions derived from it. The *hebraica veritas* has gained ground.

Although later on I will take time to analyze the limits of the concept of *hebraica veritas*, as Jerome uses it, it is right to recognize here the truth that it contains. Indeed, a philologist and translator like Jerome, *vir trilinguis*, translating from the Greek of the LXX into Latin, would not take long to feel the need to consult the terms (in this case the Hebrew ones) which were at the origin of the Greek words. In this there is little "ideology" and much experience born of the work of the translator. Frequently, words or expressions turn out to be ambiguous and the translator needs to know their meaning in order to be faithful to the work. If the work is original, the translator, like the reader, must *interpret*. If the work is a translation, it is a matter of common sense to verify the original term or terms which turn out to be ambiguous in the version, so that it is possible to identify the author's intention. In most cases this operation takes care of the ambiguity. Only in a few cases does it remain, for which reason the translator must risk an interpretation.

The need to appeal to the "original" text is even clearer when the translation is deficient or of poor quality. This is what Jerome identifies in the Greek translation of the book of Job. In this case the problem is not with the copyists but with the translator who failed to render into Greek a considerable number of verses because he did not understand them:

> Because it cannot be that those who accepted that many things had been inserted,[8] those same ones should not also confess that they were mistaken in some things, chiefly in the *Book of Job*, for if one removes from it what has been added it to it, namely, that which has been marked with asterisks, it will be largely mutilated.

7. Jerome, *Pr. Par. heb.* (*Complete Works*, II, 475).

8. Those who accept, especially on the basis of the testimony of the Hexapla, that the LXX has inserted or added many things relative to the Hebrew original.

And this only among the Greeks. But among the Latins, before the translation which we recently published with asterisks and obeli, almost seven hundred or eight hundred verses are missing,[9] so that the book, shortened and shredded and also corroded, publicly presents its ugly face to the readers.[10]

With all that has just been said, the evolution of the monk of Bethlehem in his work of translation is more than understandable, especially bearing in mind that even before he arrived in Bethlehem he knew the rudiments of Hebrew. When he undertook the task of translating from the Greek he felt ever more need to turn to the original language (Hebrew) in order not to make mistakes.[11] Since he already knew some Hebrew, it would have been easier for him to decide to go through a more systematic study of the language (and the manuscripts!) at the hands of a rabbi. Obviously, the availability, through the Hexapla, of the new Greek versions produced from the Proto-Masoretic text, facilitated and drove the task of *verifying* the original source. At the risk of oversimplifying the terms of the problem, we could conclude that Jerome's intention was not to translate from a translation but to turn to the original.

AVOIDING THE MOCKERY OF THE JEWS

A second reason at the origin of the transition which Jerome made toward the *hebraica veritas* arose, paradoxically, from his polemic with the Jews.

---

9. "Enjoy the holy Job, who among the Latins was still lying in the dung and the worms of error were swarming over him" (Jerome, *Pr. Job gr.* [*Complete Works*, II, 485]). The *Vetus Latina* was a translation of the first translation of the LXX, which had failed to translate "seven hundred or eight hundred verses" (Jerome, *Pr. Job heb* [*Complete Works*, II, 487]).

10. Jerome, *Pr. Job heb.* (*Complete Works*, II, 487).

11. One of the letters addressed to his disciple Marcela is testimony of this tension toward the Hebrew original, based on a correct understanding of the Greek and of its Latin translation, long before his turn toward the *hebraica veritas* (the letter is from the year 384): "In Hosea God threatens to take away all his graces from the fornicating people, saying: *For many days the children of Israel will be without king or prince, without sacrifice or altar, without priesthood and manifestations*. Instead of 'priesthood' and 'manifestations,' the Hebrew text has without *ephod* and without *teraphim*, as Theodotion and Symmachus also translated. Around here we understand that even in the Seventy, who translated rather in accordance with the sense than with the letter, by the *ephod* the priesthood was meant, while by *teraphim*, that is, 'images' or 'imaginations,' were understood the various works denoted by the word *teraphim*" (*Letter* 29 [*Epistolary*, I, 287–88]).

Although at some point it could be misinterpreted, *hebraica veritas* does not mean that the truth comes from the Jews. By this principle, the holy doctor was affirming that the truth contained in the Scriptures had originally been rendered in Hebrew, and more specifically in the manuscripts in Hebrew. As will be seen below, Jerome shared the same polemical tension with the Jews that moved the Christian theologians of the early centuries. And it may seem curious that in that polemic, Jerome should argue for the "original" Hebrew text.

In the first place, the argument in favor of a common starting point in the Hebrew text has as its purpose obliging the Jews to discuss the prophecies without taking refuge in the fact that their manuscripts do not say what the Christians proclaim. In his prologue to the translation of Psalms from the Hebrew, Jerome addresses Sophronius, who had encouraged the new version, as follows:

> Not long ago, while disputing with a Hebrew, you presented to him some testimonies from the *Psalms* to support the Lord as Savior and, wishing to defeat you, he assured you that almost word for word these were not found in the Hebrew text but in the passages taken from the Septuagint that you were bringing against him, you asked me with much urgency to . . . translate and prepare a new edition in the Latin language. . . .
>
> Because it is one thing to read the *Psalms* in the churches of the believers in Christ and another to respond to the Jews who slanderously criticize them word for word.[12]

The fact that this is one of the purposes of the work of translation of the holy doctor is clearly shown in the prayer with which he closes his Prologue to the book of the prophet Isaiah translated from Hebrew:

> May the One grant me the reward in the future, who knows that for this I have sweated with the learning of a foreign tongue so that the Jews would no longer insult the churches by accusing them of the falsification of the Scriptures.[13]

By translating from the Hebrew, an end is put to the taunts with which the Jews receive the versions used by the Christians, when at some points bad translations turn up:

---

12. Jerome, *Pr. Ps. heb.* (*Complete Works*, II, 493).
13. Jerome, *Pr. Isa. heb.* (*Complete Works*, II, 501).

> What we read in Isaiah: *Fortunate is he who has descendants in Zion and relatives in Jerusalem* [Isa 31:9],[14] tends to provoke the laughter of the Hebrews when they hear it, as does what is said in Amos after the description of the luxury: *They believed that these things were firm and not fleeting* [Amos 6:5]. In fact it is a rhetorical phrase and a Tullian description. But what need be done if we have as a reference the authentic books, in which neither these texts nor other similar ones are found?[15]

It should be remembered that the Jews not only abandoned the version of the LXX in clear polemic with the use that the Christians made of it, but that they came to consider its publication a tragedy, so that they established a day of fasting and mourning "in expiation for the sin committed when the Torah was spread in the language of the goyîm."[16] Curiously, Jerome, in the dispute with the Jews, does not reinforce the arguments of his opponents by emphasizing the authority of the LXX but, in a way, takes their side in order to later, from the Hebrew text, accuse them of not recognizing the fulfillment of the prophecies. The same argument is used, as will be seen below, against those Christians who criticize him for translating from the Hebrew.

THE QUOTATIONS FROM THE HEBREW OT IN THE NT: THE TRUE TESTIMONY OF THE APOSTLES

The final reason that Jerome uses to support his principle of *hebraica veritas* certainly turns out to be surprising, since it is the same one that his opponents brandish to support the *Septuaginta auctoritas*: the use that the Christian NT makes of the OT. In the prologue to the Pentateuch translated from the Hebrew, the monk of Bethlehem clearly sets out the reasons which led him to turn, in spite of the resistance of his detractors, to the *hebraica veritas*:

14. The Hebrew text says "*who has a fire in Zion and a furnace in Jerusalem.*" The initial Hebrew relative אשר in all probability has been read by the Greek translator as אשרי, "Fortunate" (μακάριος), while the term אור, "fire" must have been read as זרע, "descendants" (σπέρμα). The term οἰκείους (relatives) in the LXX seems to be derived from a translation according to the sense, parallel to σπέρμα.

15. Jerome, *Letter* 57.11 (*Epistolary*, I, 560).

16. Meg. Taʿan. 50. "Seventy elders wrote the Torah for King Ptolemy in Greek, and that day was disastrous for Israel, as was the day that they made the calf for themselves; and that is because the Law cannot be adequately translated" (Sep. Torah I:8–9). Cf. other passages in rabbinic literature in which the Greek translation is judged to be a tragedy in Barthélemy, "L'Ancien Testament a muri," 364–65.

> I was motivated by the diligence of Origen ... and, above all, by what was taught by the authority of the evangelists and apostles, in whom we read many passages taken from the Old Testament which are not in our codices, such as: *From Egypt I called my son* (Matt 2:15), and: *Because he will be called a Nazarene* (Matt 2:23), and: *They shall see the one they pierced* (John 19:37), and: *Out of his belly shall run rivers of living water* (John 7:38), and: *Things which the eye has not seen, and the ear has not heard nor have they come up to the heart of man, which God has prepared for those who love him* (1 Cor 2:9), and many other quotations which lack an appropriate *syntagma* [surrounding, context]. Let us ask them, therefore, where those passages are written and, since they will not be able to say, let us turn to the Hebraic books.[17]

Indeed, below, in the same prologue, Jerome identifies the five passages from the OT quoted in the NT that are not found in the LXX but in the Hebrew text, in order, Hos 11:1; Isa 53:2; Zech 12:10; Prov 18:4 and Isa 64:4. Let us focus on the first of the passages to verify Jerome's statement:

Matt 2:15: ἐξ Αἰγύπτου ἐκάλεσα τὸν υἱόν μου
From Egypt I called my son

Hos 11:1 (LXX): ἐξ Αἰγύπτου μετεκάλεσα τὰ τέκνα αὐτοῦ
From Egypt I called his children

Hos 11:1 (MT): וּמִמִּצְרַיִם קָרָאתִי לִבְנִי
From Egypt I called my son

As can be seen, the quotation in Matthew has not been taken from the LXX, which attests to a compound form of the verb (μετεκάλεσα) and the plural τέκνα with a third person singular possessive pronoun, but from the Hebrew text. Following his exposition, Jerome wonders what the cause is of these errors in the Greek translation of the LXX or, putting it another way, why they do not translate literally from the Hebrew text which the monk of Bethlehem knows and which prophesies Christ. The answer constitutes a new surprise:

> The Jews say that it was done based on the prudent opinion that Ptolemy, a worshiper of the only God, should not understand that also among the Hebrews there was a double divinity, a thing which they did precisely because, if they did not, it would appear that they had fallen into the doctrine of Plato. In short, wherever the

---

17. Jerome, *Pr. Pent. heb.* (*Complete Works*, II, 463).

scripture attests to something sacred about the Father, the Son and the Holy Spirit, either they translated it in another way or they completely silenced it in order to satisfy the king and not to divulge the mystery of the faith.[18]

Following the logic of Saint Jerome, the first quotation that I have analyzed, Hos 11:1, in its "original" Hebrew, attests to the call, by God, to his son. The LXX, however, has blurred this testimony of the Son, with the plural *his children*, thus avoiding the idea of a second divinity or of a divine sonship. In Jerome's view, the book of Isaiah, one of those most quoted in the NT, is paradigmatic of that attitude of the Seventy Interpreters:

> [Isaiah] should not be called a "prophet," but rather an "evangelist," for he has expounded with clarity all the mysteries of Christ and of the Church in such a way that one believes, not that he is foreseeing the future, but that he is composing a history of things past. From which I conjecture that, at that moment in time, the Seventy Interpreters were unwilling to transparently present to the gentiles the mysteries of their faith in order not to give what is holy to dogs and pearls to swine; mysteries which, when you shall read this version, you shall realize that they have been cloaked.[19]

The different passages of the OT quoted in the NT, identified by Jerome in his work as a translator,[20] seem to have been decisive in causing the monk of Bethlehem to definitively let go of the idea of the LXX as inspired translators. In the same prologue to the Pentateuch he denies the foundation of this doctrine, as it is presented in some versions of the *Letter of Aristeas*, when he states that the idea that the seventy elders translated while separated in seventy cells, and wrote (miraculously) the same words, does not belong to the original version of that letter nor does it appear

---

18. Jerome, *Pr. Pent. heb.* (*Complete Works*, II, 463). In a very similar way he argues in the prologue to his *Hebrew matters concerning Genesis*: "they [the Seventy Interpreters] were unwilling to pass on to Ptolemy, king of Alexandria, the mystical matters that are found in the Holy Scriptures, especially those which promised the coming of Christ, so that it would not appear that the Jews too worshiped another God: for to them that disciple of Plato attributed great importance on account of this, because it was said that they worshiped a single God" (Jerome, *Qu. hebr. Gen.* [*Complete Works*, IV, 7]).

19. Jerome, *Pr. Isa. heb.* (*Complete Works*, II, 499).

20. In *Letter 57 to Pammachius, on the art of translating well*, Jerome develops the five passages of the OT cited above and adds others where he shows that the authors of the NT used the Hebrew text and not the LXX (cf. *Letter* 57.7–11 [*Epistolary*, I, 550–61]).

in Josephus' testimony about it.[21] On the contrary, Aristeas and Josephus, speaking of the seventy translators,

> They write that they were gathered in a royal palace, not that they had prophesied, for it is one thing to be a diviner [*vatem*] and another to be a translator [*interpretem*]: in the former case the spirit predicts what is to come; in the latter, erudition and the wealth of words translates what it understands, unless, perchance, it is to be believed that . . . the Holy Spirit dictated with some words the passages of the same books by the mouths of the Seventy Interpreters and with other words by the mouths of the apostles [that is, the quotations of the OT in the NT], so that what the former kept silent, the latter lied by saying that it was written.[22]

Jerome's argumentation in support of the *hebraica veritas*, which in this prologue reaches its final stage, closes by placing his Latin translation from the Hebrew on a level with that of the LXX, and even above it, since he is a Christian and better recognizes, inasmuch as it has already taken place, that which before Christ might have been ambiguous:

> They translated before the coming of Christ and what they did not know, they expressed with ambiguous statements; but we, after His passion and resurrection, write not so much prophecy as history, for in the one way are told things that are heard, and in the other, things that are seen: that which we understand better, we also express better.[23]

Contrary to what his detractors argue, the authority of the apostles is what leads Jerome to set aside the LXX and embrace the *hebraica veritas*:

> Hear, then, competitor; detractor, listen: I do not condemn, I do not reprimand the Seventy, but, with confidence, rather than all of them I prefer the apostles. For me Christ rings through the mouths of the latter, whom I read placed before the Prophets with respect to spiritual charisms, among whom the Interpreters are on the penultimate step.[24]

21. Josephus, *A.J.* 12.2.
22. Jerome, *Pr. Pent. heb.* (*Complete Works*, II, 465).
23. Jerome, *Pr. Pent. heb.* (*Complete Works*, II, 465).
24. Jerome, *Pr. Pent. heb.* (*Complete Works*, II, 465). About the "penultimate step," cf. 1 Cor 12:28–30: "Some people God has designated in the church to be, first, apostles; second, prophets; third, teachers; then, mighty deeds; then gifts of healing, assistance, administration, and varieties of tongues. Are all apostles? Are all prophets? Are all teachers? Do all work mighty deeds? Do all have gifts of healing? Do all speak in tongues? Do all interpret?"

CHAPTER 4

The *Hebraica Veritas*
Shadows

UP TO THIS POINT we have see the arguments in favor of the *hebraica veritas*, as Jerome presents them, at the same time that I have highlighted their relevance: the pull toward the original of a work (as opposed to its translation), the possibility of having available the same text that the Jews use in order to facilitate discussion with them, and access to the original text of the OT that the apostles quoted in the NT.

Now is the time to bring to light the weaknesses of the argumentation of the holy doctor. It is necessary to recognize that today we have a knowledge of the textual history of the OT, in its transmission in both Hebrew and Greek, which Jerome did not possess and which facilitates our critical labor.

WHERE IS THE "ORIGINAL" TEXT?

The first criticism that it is necessary to address to the Dalmatian is that the Hebrew manuscripts available to him, coming from the Jews of Palestine, cannot be considered "the" *hebraica veritas* understood as the original text of the books of the OT from which the LXX translated. Indeed, today we know that the Hebrew text that was circulating in the time of Jerome was no more than *one* text type, specifically the Proto-Masoretic, that is, the unvocalized Hebrew text that must have been standardized in about the second century C.E. in Palestine and became normative for Pharisaic

The Hebraica Veritas: Shadows

rabbinic Judaism, the only survivor (together with "messianic" or Christian Judaism) of the disasters of 68–70 C.E. (destruction of the Essene settlement of Qumran; destruction of the temple and disappearance of the Sadducees) and 135 C.E. (final disappearance of the Zealots at the hands of the Romans following the Bar Kokhba revolt).

If we go back to at least the second century B.C.E., the predecessor of the Proto-Masoretic text type, namely the Pre-Masoretic, lived side by side with two other Hebrew text types that could equally well claim for themselves the title of *hebraica veritas*: the Samaritan Pentateuch and the Hebrew *Vorlage* of the LXX (that is, the Hebrew text that underlies the Greek translation).

Once this textual panorama is assimilated, it becomes obvious that consideration of the *pluses* and *minuses* of the LXX, in relation to the Hebrew text of which Jerome is making use, as "errors" or as "distortions," as "additions" or as "omissions," must be revised. It is true that there are numerous cases in which the LXX start with a Hebrew *Vorlage* shared with the Proto-Masoretic text and produce an erroneous translation,[1] or because of a lack of skill, ignorance or carelessness they omit words or verses,[2] or they resort to interpretive paraphrases as a solution when faced with a difficult text.[3]

---

1. In Deut 4:34 and 26:8 the Hebrew text uses the expression "great fear" (מורא גדל), which accompanies the powerful intervention of God to liberate his people from Egypt. The Greek translator committed a very understandable error: deriving מורא from the root ראה, "to see," and not from the root ירא, "to fear," thus translating it as "great visions."

2. In 1 Sam 23:11–12 the Hebrew text says, "[v. 11] 'Will the leading citizens of Keilah deliver me into the hands of Saul? Will Saul come down as your servant has heard? Lord, God of Israel, make it known, please, to your servant.' The Lord answered: 'He will come down.' [v. 12] David repeated: 'Will the leading citizens of Keilah deliver me together with my men into the hand of Saul?' The Lord answered: 'They will deliver you.'" In the Greek translation of the LXX v. 12 does not exist and the final answer of the Lord in v. 11 is "They will deliver you" and not "He will come down." Clearly the Greek translator has committed an error by jumping from the first "The Lord answered" (ויאמר יהוה) (v. 11) to the second (v. 12) and omitting a whole verse.

3. In Gen 4:7 God addresses a Cain who is dejected by the fact that the Lord has not looked favorably on his offering. The Hebrew text says, "Would you not be encouraged if you did what is good? But if you do not do good, sin is crouching at the door and is greedy for you, although you will be able to master it." The text is problematic because God gives no reason for why the offering of Cain, made according to the Law, is worse than that of Abel. The translation of the LXX is a clear interpretation which resolves the problem: "Is it not true that, although you have made the correct offerings, if you have not divided correctly, you have sinned? Calm down; its inclination tends toward you, and you will master it."

However, on many other occasions, the differences between the LXX and the Hebrew manuscripts from which Jerome was translating have to do with different Hebrew text types. In this case it is hard to discern which Hebrew text is the "original" and which is "secondary," if in fact we are not looking at different editions of a single Hebrew text, in which case the question about the original text and the secondary one makes no sense, as happens in the book of Jeremiah (we should rather speak of a first and second edition).

WHEN THE GREEK TEXT IS SUPERIOR TO THE HEBREW

The second criticism addressed to Jerome's argumentation has to do with his wish to start with a text shared with the Jews in order to provoke discussions, and even more, to support Christian apologetics. This *desideratum* of the holy doctor is based on a presupposition which I have already criticized: in Jerome's view there exists a single Hebrew original text, which coincides with the one attested in the manuscripts of the Jews, and from which the Greek translation of the LXX departs. The monk of Bethlehem wished to do away with the mockery of the Jews (in reaction to translations of the LXX which diverged from the Proto-Masoretic) by setting aside a version which, at times, attests to a Hebrew text that is better or at least an alternative, if not a different edition.

I will give an example in which the LXX preserves a "better" text than the one attested in the Hebrew manuscripts that Saint Jerome was using. Psalm 145 is an acrostic, that is, a poem in which each verse begins with a consonant of the alphabet, in an orderly and progressive form. Both in the Hebrew manuscripts of Jerome's time and in the later Masoretic tradition, this Psalm has twenty-one verses and not twenty-two as would be expected in an acrostic poem (there are twenty-two letters in the Hebrew alphabet). Indeed, the verse corresponding to the consonant *nun* is missing. In the Greek version of the LXX, as well as in the Syriac of the Peshitta, there is one more verse, precisely the one that follows the verse in Hebrew which begins with the consonant *mem* (the consonant that precedes *nun*). By following Jerome's argumentation, the Jews could mock the Christians for "adding" something that is not in the Hebrew manuscripts. This is so much so that in his Latin translation of the Psalter *iuxta Hebraeos*, Jerome follows the Hebrew composition of twenty-one verses. The appearance in the caves of Qumran of the 11QPs[a] manuscript of Psalms has resolved a problem

The Hebraica Veritas: Shadows

which in reality was already quite clear. That manuscript (copied around the first half of the first century C.E.) contains Psalm 145 in Hebrew with twenty-two verses, including the one that begins with *nun*. In this case the LXX must have preserved the original form of a Psalm which in the Proto-Masoretic tradition must have accidentally lost a verse.

WHEN THE NT QUOTES FROM THE VERSION OF THE LXX

A third and final criticism affects the consideration, on Jerome's part, of the Hebrew text as the source used by the apostles to quote the OT in the NT. It is necessary to recognize in the holy doctor a keen spirit to get around an argument of his detractors and great textual expertise for identifying the passages on which to support himself. Indeed, Jerome is right when he shows passages in which the authors of the NT base themselves on the Hebrew text and not on the Greek of the LXX for their quotations from the OT. However, he omits the fact that in many other passages the quoted text comes from the LXX, when the latter attest to a form different from the Proto-Masoretic.[4]

Indeed, the development of textual studies around the MT, LXX and the Greek NT has made it possible for us to know in greater detail the sources of the quotations of the OT in the NT.[5] Obviously these sources vary from one book to another and even, at times, within each book. Certainly there is a small percentage of quotations taken from the (Pre-Masoretic) Hebrew text when it diverges from the Greek of the LXX, as Jerome made a point of showing, which is rather notable in the quotations of fulfillment

---

4. Actually, Jerome accepts the fact that there are passages in the NT in which the quotations follow the LXX, but these are, in his opinion, places in which the Greek text does not differ from the Hebrew. In one of his letters, after speaking of the passages which the LXX have omitted in relation to the Hebrew text, he adds: "However, the version of the Seventy has quite properly prevailed in the churches, whether because it is the first and ran even before the coming of Christ, or because it was used by the apostles, although only when it does not disagree with the Hebrew" (*Letter* 57.11 [*Epistolary*, I, 560]).

5. In this respect great utility can be derived from the multi-volume work of Hans Hübner, *Vetus Testamentum in Novo*, which presents in columns the Greek text of the NT (where it refers to the OT) and its parallels in the Bible of the LXX, MT, *et alia*.

in the gospel of Matthew.⁶ Even so, it can be affirmed that in most cases the quotations from the OT come from the Greek version of the LXX.⁷

It is hard to conclude that Jerome did not realize, on the basis of his work as a translator from the Greek and from the Hebrew, that many of the quotations from the OT in the NT followed the textual form of the LXX when it departed from the (Proto-Masoretic) Hebrew text. Moreover, in the prologue to the Latin translation of Chronicles from the Hebrew, speaking precisely of the quotations mentioned, he says:

> Of course, the apostles and the evangelists knew the Seventy Interpreters, but from where do they get what is not contained in the Seventy Interpreters?⁸

From this statement it can be seen that Jerome was aware that the NT quoted sometimes according to the LXX and other times according to the Hebrew text available to him. So it seems the monk of Bethlehem drew exaggerated conclusions with regard to the will of the Seventy Interpreters to blur the mysteries of the faith present in the Hebrew text in order not to scandalize the gentiles.

Actually, Jerome's argument turns against him. Indeed, his decision to translate the OT from the Hebrew, thus replacing the previous translation from the Greek, entailed stealing from the Latin-language Christians all those passages of the old Scripture which the NT had quoted from the LXX, when they did not agree with the Hebrew Proto-Masoretic text. Numerous passages could be quoted, as the holy doctor does in the opposite direction. One will suffice to illustrate, specifically from the gospel from which Jerome takes his first example, that of Matthew. In this way we see how the evangelist who uses the Hebrew text for the so-called "fulfillment quotations" turns to the LXX on many other occasions.

In Matt 13:14–15 the evangelist quotes Isa 6:9–10, which has some major differences in its forms in Hebrew and in the Greek of the LXX. These differences are shown in italics:⁹

> MT: And he said: "Go and tell this people: '*Hear* well, but do not understand; *see* well, but do not comprehend.' *Dull* the heart of

---

6. Cf. Menken, *Matthew's Bible*.
7. Cf. Kraus, "Septuagint Quotations."
8. Jerome, *Pr. Par. heb.* (*Complete Works*, II, 475).
9. I follow the exposition of the problem of the reception of Isa 6:9–10 in the NT given by Jódar, "Is 6,9–10."

The Hebraica Veritas: Shadows

this people, *make it* hard of hearing and *close* its eyes; so that it may not see with its eyes or hear with its ears nor may its heart understand, and it should be converted and *it should be healed*."

LXX: And he said: "Go and tell this people: 'You *shall hear* with your ear and you shall not understand, and *you shall look* well and you shall not hear.' *For* the heart of this people *has become dull*, with difficulty *they listened* with their ears and *they closed* their eyes, in order not to see with their eyes and not to hear with their ears and understand with their heart and be converted and that *I should heal them*."

In this parallel presentation it can well be seen that the differences are substantial, especially with regard to the one responsible for the blindness of the people, which in the MT is the prophet and in the LXX the stubbornness of the people themselves. So then, Matt 13:14–15 follows the Greek text of the LXX point by point: Jesus speaks to them in parables so that the freedom of each one may come to light.

I will leave for later the discussion about the quotation of Isa 7:14 in Matt 1:22–23 ("All this happened so that what the Lord had said through the prophet would be fulfilled: 'Look: the Virgin shall conceive and will bear a son and they will give him the name Emmanuel, which means God-with-us'"), since it is relevant for the defense of the *Septuaginta auctoritas*. Suffice it here to say that Jerome takes it for granted that in the Hebrew text of Isa 7:14 virgin should be read and not simply damsel.[10] In fact, in the Vulgate, he translated from the Hebrew into Latin as "ecce virgo concipiet."

Nothing indicates that Jerome could have known a Hebrew text that did not have the term עלמה, "young damsel." In fact, the monk of Bethlehem must have known the translation νεᾶνις (*young damsel*) of the Hebrew term made by the new Greek versions sponsored by the Jews, Aquila, Symmachus, and Theodotion, just as he must have known the polemic that had arisen with the Jews on the basis of the translation παρθένος, *virgin*, in the LXX.[11] To translate עלמה as *virgo* indicates a use, unconfessed on the part of Saint Jerome, of a principle which is not that of *hebraica veritas*.

---

10. So he writes, with regard to this quotation, in the letter *To Pammachius, on the art of translating well*: "Porro in Hebraeo ita scriptum legimus: 'ecce virgo concipiet'" (*Letter* 57.8 [*Epistolary*, I, 554]).

11. Already Justin, in his *Dialogue with Trypho the Jew* (written between 155 and 160 C.E.), attests to this polemic (cf. *Dial.* 43.8; 67.1; 68.7; 71.3; 84.3). A little later, Irenaeus also refers to the same problem (cf. *Haer.* III, 21.1–4).

CHAPTER 5

The *Septuaginta Auctoritas*
Lights

I WILL MOVE ON now to study the second principle in tension, the *Septuaginta auctoritas*. This same Latin expression is frequently employed by Augustine, especially when what is at stake is the text of the OT which should serve as the starting point. In his correspondence with Jerome, the bishop of Hippo explicitly says that he does not want the translation that Jerome had done from the Hebrew to be read in the churches "in order not to lessen the authority of the Seventy" (*ne contra Septuaginta auctoritatem*).[1] In his work *City of God* he dedicates some chapters of book XVIII precisely to laying the foundation for the role of the version of the LXX in the life of the Church by basing himself on the marvelous history of the translation, as it is told in the legend of Aristeas. The title of chapter forty-three is very significant in this sense: "Authority of the Seventy Interpreters, who, apart from the honor of the Hebrew style, must be preferred to all the translators" (*De auctoritate Septuaginta interpretum, quae, salvo honore hebraei stili, omnibus sit interpretibus praeferenda*).[2]

Below I will expound the reasons that guided Augustine in his defense of the authority of the LXX in the face of the movement in favor of the *hebraica veritas* that was taking place in Jerome. Obviously, Augustine was not the first or only one who claimed this authority for the Greek translation. Nevertheless, because he was a contemporary of Jerome it was to him

---

1. Augustine, *Letter* 116.35 (*Epistolary*, II, 353).
2. Augustine, *Civ.* 18.43.

that it fell to defend the principle in the context of the translation that the monk of Bethlehem was doing from the Hebrew. Therefore, I will start with his reasons, although on occasion I will have them hinge on the arguments of the Christian theologians who preceded him or I will show their continuity over time through the reflections of recent authors.

As I have already done in the study of the other principle at stake, I will first present the reasons in favor of the authority of the LXX, with everything that may be valid about them, while leaving the weaknesses of the argumentation for a later time.

In an effort at synthesis, I will divide the reasons in favor of the authority of the LXX into three groups:

THE CHRISTIAN BIBLE, THE BIBLE OF THE APOSTLES

After introducing the translation of the LXX, Saint Augustine, in his *De civitate Dei*, recognizes that there are other Greek versions made from the Hebrew, specifically Aquila, Symmachus, Theodotion, and "in addition, another version, by an unknown author, and lacking the name of the translator, it is called the 'fifth edition.'" To the question that could arise for his readers about which version to read, the teacher from Hippo adds:

> However, the Church received this from the Seventy as if it were the only one, and the Christian Greeks make use of it, most of whom do not know whether there is another one. From this version of the Seventy was made the translation into Latin of the text that the Latin churches use. Although in our days the presbyter Jerome, a man so wise and expert in the three languages, translated the same Scriptures into Latin, not from the Greek, but from the Hebrew. The Jews, even though they confess that their literary effort is truthful, claim that the Seventy Interpreters made mistakes in many things. However, the Churches of Christ think that no one should place himself ahead of the authority of these men, chosen then by the pontiff Eleazar for work of such a caliber.[3]

Augustine's statements are strong and, although they have the support of tradition, in this case they take on greater gravity because they are made after the initiative of Jerome, who was certainly no minor theologian, much less a heretic. The new translation from the Hebrew by the monk of Bethlehem, the man of great prestige whom the pope Saint Damasus had

---

3. Augustine, *Civ.* 18.43.

charged with the revision of the Latin version of the gospels, comprised the first serious threat to the authority which until that time had been vested in the Seventy Interpreters.

With the authority of a bishop, Augustine states that the Church received the version of the LXX "as if it were the only one" (*tamquam sola esset*), so much so that the Greek churches (directly) and the Latin ones (by means of a translation), that is, the whole Christian world for the one from Hippo, do not use (or even know of) another one. In case that did not make it clear, the statement takes on a solemn tone to conclude that "the *Churches of Christ* think that no one should place himself ahead of the *authority* of these men."

The reference to the Jews in this passage from *De civitate Dei* turns out to be significant. It does not escape Augustine that the version of the LXX is a work by Jewish interpreters and that the Hebrews read the Scriptures in their original language. These are things which, in dialogue with Jerome, he had learned not to discount.[4] However, the use which the Christians made of the LXX led the Jews to state that "the Seventy Interpreters made mistakes in many things," to the point that they rejected their own translation and made new Greek versions. In this way, the version of the LXX, rejected by the Jews, came to be *the* Christian Bible, while the Hebrew manuscripts came to be *the* Jewish Bible.

The information that Augustine passes on to us is well founded: in different places in the rabbinic literature there are lists of the alterations which the LXX presumably introduced into the Greek translation of the Hebrew Torah. In total, and depending on the sources, between eleven and eighteen changes are listed (in the Pentateuch alone).[5] Today it is known that the distrust, on the part of the Jews of Palestine, toward the Greek version done in Alexandria already existed before the appearance of the Christians.

Indeed, the *Letter of Aristeas* presents itself as an apologetic document to support the prestige of the LXX in the face of the authority of the Hebrew text. The correction of the original translation to bring it closer

---

4. Cf. *Letter* 116.34 (from Augustine to Jerome) (*Epistolary*, I, 351–52). In the final part of this study I will refer to the continuation of *Civ.* 18.43, where it is noted that the dialogue with Jerome has opened the bishop of Hippo to a greater consideration of the Hebrew text. Cf. La Bonnardière, "Augustin," 307–12.

5. To learn about the rabbinic sources and the passages listed, together with a textual study of them, cf. Tov, "Rabbinic Tradition." Cf. also Wasserstein and Wasserstein, *Legend of the Septuagint*, 51–94.

to the Hebrew was a process that began long before Aquila, and without any relation to the Christians. The discovery in the caves of the Dead Sea (specifically *Naḥal Ḥever*) of a scroll which contains fragments of a Greek version of the Twelve Prophets (8HevXIIgr), dated between 50 B.C.E. and 50 C.E., with notable differences in relation to the LXX, has revolutionized our knowledge of the Jewish revisions. Barthélemy describes it as a systematic revision of the LXX on the basis of a Hebrew manuscript of the Proto-Masoretic type.[6]

The use which the Christians began to make of the LXX, highlighting the prophecies of Christ that are contained in it, together with the fact that the dominant Judaism came to coincide with Pharisaic rabbinism, definitively distanced this Greek version from Jewish orthodoxy. In this way the two worlds were separated, the Jewish and the Christian, with two languages (Hebrew and Greek) and two different Bibles (Hebrew Proto-Masoretic and Greek Septuagint).

But the Bible of the LXX was not simply the Scripture of the Christians because of that fact that it was *the* Greek translation available in the synagogues of the Mediterranean when the followers of Christ were expanding through a world dominated by the Koine. It is above all, following the argumentation of Augustine, the *Bible of the apostles*, and more specifically the Scriptures used by them. In one of his letters to Jerome, in the context of the umpteenth discussion about the status of the Hebrew text and the Greek translation, Augustine says with regard to the version of the LXX that "it is not small, the authority of the latter, which has managed to become so widespread, and *which the apostles have used* (*et qua usos apostolos*), as reality itself proves, and as I recall you yourself testify."[7]

What does it mean that the Septuagint has been *used* by the apostles? Augustine is referring, obviously, to the use which the NT makes of the Greek version when it quotes the OT.[8] The fact that the apostles (that is, the authors of the NT) had turned to the LXX to quote the Scriptures was a piece of information uncontroversially acquired and transmitted among

---

6. Cf. Barthélemy, *Devanciers d'Aquila*; Barthélemy, "Redécouverte."

7. Augustine, *Letter* 104.6 (*Epistolary*, II, 144). Speaking of the Christian people who read the version of the LXX, Augustine says that their ears and hearts "are accustomed to hearing that translation, which, moreover, *was approved by the apostles* (*ab apostolis abprobata est*)" (*Letter* 116.35 [*Epistolary*, II, 353]).

8. In Augustine's statement, "and the apostles have used it, as *reality itself* demonstrates," the expression *res ipsa* (*reality itself*) refers to the verifiable data, that is, to the manuscripts of each book of the NT compared with those of the LXX.

Christian authors up until Jerome.⁹ As has already been seen, the monk of Bethlehem, on the basis of some quotations in the NT, calls this into question and even turns the argument around to affirm that the apostles used the Hebrew text.

I have already had occasion to observe that Jerome is partial in this judgment and, very probably, unfaithful to the data that he himself had available. Even so, his statement had the virtue of putting before everyone a piece of information that was little known until that time: a portion of the quotations of the OT in the NT come from the Hebrew text when the latter differs from the LXX. At the same time, the statement of the Dalmatian makes it necessary to verify the hypothesis received in the tradition about the use of the LXX in the NT. Can it continue to be supported? I have previously alluded to the modern textual studies which have shown the complexity of the problem of the quotations but which have confirmed the dominant position of the version of the LXX in the NT, at least in relation to the Proto-Masoretic Hebrew tradition.

Again, a single example will suffice to illustrate why it had been obvious to the Christian tradition of the early centuries that the apostles had *used* the LXX.¹⁰ In Acts 2:22–36 we are presented with the speech of Peter in which he announces to the people that Jesus of Nazareth, whom they supposed was dead, had been resurrected and had been made Lord and Messiah. God had freed him from death, says Peter, as had been prophesied by David (namely, in the Psalms). In that context Psalm 16:8–11 (15:8–11 according to the LXX) is quoted at length. Peter's whole insistence is on the fact that Jesus, who has gone into the grave (or pit), has not known the consequent corruption (of the flesh). He bases himself for this on Ps 16:10 according to the LXX, which states that "your holy one" (taken as Christ, the holy one of God) "will not experience *corruption* [διαφθορά]." The Hebrew text uses, instead of the term *corruption*, the word *pit* (שחת), which would not have "worked" in the apostle's argumentation because of the simple fact that Jesus did know the pit, that is, the grave:

> LXX: Because you will not abandon my soul to Hades nor will you allow your holy one to see *corruption*.
>
> MT: Because you will not abandon my soul to Sheol nor will you allow your holy one to see the *pit*.

9. Cf. Barthélemy "Place de la Septante"; Veltri, "L'ispirazione della LXX."
10. Cf. other examples in Kraus, "Septuagint Quotations," 631–36; McLay, *Use of the Septuagint*.

I will now move ahead in the argumentation in favor of the *Septuaginta auctoritas* based, precisely, on the testimony of the NT. At base this is a reason in favor of the LXX which is also derived from the statement that the Septuagint is the Bible used by the apostles.

THE *PRAEPARATIO EVANGELICA*

The Interpretation of the LXX, Foundation of the Theology of the NT

The example I utilized to illustrate the use of the LXX in the NT helps us to understand that the appeal to this Greek version on the part of the "apostles," in the understanding of Augustine and the rest of the Christian theologians of the early centuries, goes beyond the identification of one textual source (the Greek Septuagint) instead of another (Hebrew Proto-Masoretic). In many of the quotations taken from the LXX (when they differ from the Hebrew text then known) what is at stake is the theology of the NT, the theological foundations of Christianity. In these cases, the arguments that are carried out based on the authority of the Scriptures would have been impossible on the basis of the Hebrew Proto-Masoretic text. Said in a positive way, a certain form of expression of the LXX (however it may be regarded in relation to the Hebrew text) turns out to be *providential* for the birth of Christian theology. In this sense, the LXX (including its process of translation and its textual vicissitudes) could be spoken of as a *praeparatio evangelica*.[11]

Augustine himself attributes to divine Providence those parts of the LXX, accepted by the NT, which are not found in the Hebrew manuscripts and which were appropriately translated, with the guidance of the Holy Spirit, for the instruction of the gentiles predestined to the faith:

11. At the beginning of the fourth century C.E., the apologetic work of Eusebius of Caesarea, Εὐαγγελικὴ προπαρασκευή (*praeparatio evangelica* in Latin), had "popularized" an expression that goes back to the second century C.E. Even so, its content varies from some authors to others. It can refer to the preparation that the divine Mystery has made in the Greek culture and authors, in view of the arrival of Christ (cf. "the seeds of the word" in the *Apologia* of Justin [cf. *2 Apol.*, 13.2–6] or Greek philosophy as "preparation" to reach Christ in the *Stromata* of Clement of Alexandria [cf. *Strom.* 1.28.1–3; 1.37.1–6]), to the providential antecedents of Greek philosophy in the wisdom of the Hebrews (this is how, in large part, it is used by Eusebius and by Clement of Alexandria himself) or to the role of the Greek translation of the LXX in the economy of salvation (so it appears in book VIII of Eusebius' *Praep. ev.*). Cf. Bertram, "Praeparatio evangelica."

> Therefore, even though in the Hebrew copies there may be found something different from what the latter [the LXX] wrote, I judge that it should be attributed to divine Providence (*divinae dispensationi*) executed through them, so that the books which the Jewish people did not want to make known, because of religion or because of envy of the other nations, should be delivered so long in advance, through the ministry of King Ptolemy, to the gentiles who were to believe in the Lord. Therefore, it was possible for them to translate in the way that the Holy Spirit judged would be suitable to the gentiles.[12]

In Augustine's view, therefore, the version of the LXX belongs to the designs of Providence, which willed that the Bible should be translated into Greek with a view to the entrance of the pagan peoples into the Church. It was not just a matter of making the Scriptures available in the lingua franca when Christianity began to expand. Augustine was referring to those passages peculiar to the LXX that were recognized as prophetic of the coming of Christ by the NT. I will give an example which will prove especially illuminating and will take us into the providential role of the LXX in the origins of Christianity.

The letter to the Hebrews plays a decisive role in the Christology of the NT. It is the canonical document that presents Christ as high priest. Bearing in mind that Jesus is not from a priestly family but from the tribe of David, the letter to the Hebrews derives the priesthood of Christ from the rite of Melchizedek (Heb 5:5–7 refers to Ps 110:4 and Gen 14:17–20). The document takes time to illustrate this surprising priesthood: the parallelism with Melchizedek, the eternal priesthood, the new temple, the new covenant, etc. Throughout the argumentation the OT plays a fundamental role; it is quoted extensively, almost in the manner of Midrash,[13] especially the Psalms,[14] in most cases according to the version of the LXX.

Now in the tenth chapter, the letter presents the sacrifice of Jesus. After all, a priest carries out his ministry by offering sacrifices for his own sins and for those of the people. What is the sacrifice that Jesus offers? At

---

12. Augustine, *Doctr. chr.* 2.15.22.
13. Cf. Tönges, "Epistle to the Hebrews."
14. This is the book that is used most in the letter, with fourteen quotations, among which stand out, because of their importance in the argumentation or because of the length of the reference, Pss 8:4–6; 40:6–8; 45:6–7; 95:7–11; 102:25–27; 110:1, 4. Cf. Belli et al., *Vetus in Novo*, 212–13.

this point the letter brings in the dialogue between the Father and the Son when the latter comes into the world:

> For it is impossible that the blood of bulls and male goats should take away sins. Therefore, when he enters the world he says: *You did not want sacrifices or offerings, but you formed a body for me* [σῶμα δὲ κατηρτίσω μοι]; *you did not accept holocausts or expiatory offerings. Then I said: See, I am coming—for thus it is written at the beginning of the book about me—to do, oh God, your will.* (Heb 10:4–7)

I have highlighted in italics the long quotation from Psalm 40:7–9 (Ps 39 LXX) which the author of the letter gives. The Psalm is put in the mouth of the Son, who addresses the Father at the moment when he takes on human flesh to enter into the world. Jesus does not offer sacrifices, offerings, holocausts or expiatory offerings but the very body which the Father has given him. He will offer it on the cross for the sins of the world. In this very first Christian theological reflection, the textual form of the LXX turns out to be providential. Indeed, the Hebrew text of Ps 40:7 says, "You did not want sacrifices or offerings, but *you have opened my ear* [אזנים כרית לי]," while the LXX, with unanimity in its Greek textual tradition, reads, "You did not want sacrifices or offerings, but *you formed a body for me* [σῶμα δὲ κατηρτίσω μοι]."[15]

Even today there is argument about this *crux interpretum*. It is hard to decide which reading ("ear" or "body") has precedence in a hypothetical

---

15. Surprisingly, the critical edition of the Septuagint of Psalms from Göttingen, done by A. Rahlfs in 1939, proposes as "original text" ὠτία δὲ κατηρτίσω μοι, when the term ὠτία ("ears") is not attested in any Greek manuscript (except, obviously, in the late versions of Aquila, Symmachus, and Theodotion—the testimony of which has come down to us through the marginal annotations of the Syro-Hexapla—who are translating from a Proto-Masoretic text). Rahlfs considers that the reading σῶμα must have come into the manuscript tradition because of the influence of Heb 10:5. He gives precedence to ὠτία because the Vulgate *iuxta Septuaginta* and a Latin manuscript of the *Vetus* (La^G, sixth century C.E.), which in theory are translating from a Greek text, alone read *aures*. In my opinion, both Latin readings could be understood as a contamination on the basis of the Hexaplaric works. *Pace* Rahlfs, the fifth column of Origen's Hexapla reads σῶμα, and not ὠτία, according to the indirect testimony of the Syro-Hexapla (which translate as ܦܓܪܐ, *body*). Speaking of the need for a new edition of the book of Psalms in the LXX, Martin Karrer states: "Individual NT quotations will need to be corrected: σῶμα in Ps 39:7 LXX is consistently witnessed by the main manuscripts, in the Antiochene text and in Heb 10:6, so Rahlfs' decision for ὠτία is no longer satisfactory" (Karrer, "Septuagint Text," 622). Cf. Steyn, *Quest*, 282–97; Rusen-Weinhold, *Septuagintapsalter* (especially chapter IV.3 "Die Psalmzitate im Neuen Testament. Der Hebräerbrief").

genealogical tree, or to put it another way, which would be the original reading and which the secondary.[16] What is obvious is that the author of the letter to the Hebrews recognized in this Psalm, as in others, in the form of the LXX, a prophecy of the Incarnation and the sacrifice of Christ on the cross. Thus it can be said that the OT, in its Greek reception, turns out to be providential for canonical and inspired reflection on Christ.[17]

The Dialogue between Julius Africanus and Origen: An Antecedent of the Present Polemic

To catch in action the awareness that the first Christian theologians had of the providential role of the LXX, it can be very advantageous to approach the epistolary exchange that Julius Africanus and Origen had around the year 248.[18] This dialogue has the virtue, moreover, of providing an antecedent to the polemic between Jerome and Augustine about the status of the Hebrew and Greek texts of the OT. The African writes to Origen to show him his perplexity about the fact that the Alexandrian has publicly used the story of Susanna (Dan 13) when it should be considered, in his opinion, a recent and false writing, which probably does not belong to the Scriptures. Among other reasons, the African argues that this story is not found in the manuscripts of the Jews and, in addition, it has some plays on words in Greek which prove that it was not translated from Hebrew, as, on the other hand, the rest of the holy books have been.

Origen's response, and thus its interest for us, opens up the problem that the African poses for the whole OT. With the expertise to be found

---

16. Pierre Grelot thinks that the Greek reading σῶμα, *body*, did not exist in the manuscripts of the LXX before Christ. It was probably introduced in the great codices of the fourth century C.E. because of the influence of the reading of the letter to the Hebrews (Heb 10:5). However, he does not justify his hypothesis nor does he resolve the problem, but rather transfers it to the letter to the Hebrews: Why did its author modify the Psalm in such a radical way? Cf. Grelot, "Texte du Psaume 39,7." The most conclusive datum is that the Greek manuscript tradition unanimously attests σῶμα, including the most recently discovered manuscripts, especially the *Bodmer* papyrus XXIV (Rahlfs 2110; third/fourth century C.E.).

17. Another paradigmatic case is that of the Pauline letters, where a good part of the theological reflection is at stake. In them Paul constantly bases himself on the OT in its Greek form in the LXX, which frequently departs from the Hebrew text. Cf. Wagner, *Heralds*.

18. Cf. the edition of the Greek text with a French translation by Nicholas de Lange in *Philocalie*.

in one who has for years been engaged in the critical work of the Hexapla, Origen presents to him different passages of the Scriptures in which the Hebrew text and the Greek ecclesiastical one differ. Thus he mentions other "deuterocanonical" passages of Daniel (Greek additions to chapter 3; the story of Bel and the Dragon: Dan 14), the Greek parts of Esther, various passages in Job, textual differences in Jeremiah and some differences in Genesis and Exodus.

He culminates his reasoning with a rhetorical question which goes to the heart of the present discussion and which justifies the aforementioned parallelism with the correspondence between Jerome and Augustine:

> In order not to be ignorant of all these data, would we have to eliminate the copies [ἀντίγραφα] used by the churches and order the community to reject the sacred books that are used in it, only to honor the Jews and persuade them to hand over to us the pure texts which they possess, free from every addition [τῶν καθαρῶν καὶ μηδὲν πλάσμα ἐχόντων]?[19]

Origen here takes to the extreme the logic of his interlocutor.[20] We do not know to what degree the African might feel himself to be recognized in a conclusion like this one (that is, if he would respond affirmatively to Origen's question). What is clear is that, 150 years later, Origen's rhetorical question was taken seriously by Jerome and, to the outrage of Augustine, he turned it into a publishing project: a Latin translation of the OT that would only contain the *hebraica veritas* attested by the manuscripts of the Jews.

Both Origen's question and Jerome's project were possible because the huge work which the Alexandrian carried out in his Hexapla made Christian theologians aware of the magnitude and importance of the textual differences between the Greek text available to the Church and the Hebrew which the Jews read. Origen was the first one to become aware of their nature and extent. More than a century would have to pass before the textual instrument of the Alexandrian would spread and the awareness of those differences would generate a debate like the one that Jerome and Augustine had, with decisive consequences for the future of the Bible in the West.[21]

---

19. Origen, *Ep. Afr.* 8.
20. Cf. Barthélemy, "Origène et le texte," 249.
21. Barthélemy believes that Origen's disciples did not understand the purpose of his Hexapla and considered that the books not shared by the Jews were outside of the canon. In his opinion, this prepared the ground for Jerome's radicalism. To confront Jerome "il eût fallu un homme de l'érudition d'Origène. Il ne se trouva qu'Augustin. Le vieux

But Origen's question was only rhetorical. In fact, his position was very far from the one that Jerome would later take. In the answer that he gives himself, he rejects as a temptation the argument of the African which he himself had taken to the extreme:

> But then, would it perchance be necessary to admit that Providence, which seeks, through the Holy Scriptures, the edification of all the churches of Christ, has not concerned itself with "those who were purchased at a great price," "for whom Christ has died," whom "God," who is love, "did not spare," "but delivered him up for all of us," so that "with him all things might be given to us"? On account of all this, consider whether it is not worthwhile to remember concerning it: "Do not move the eternal boundaries which your fathers set."[22]

With this answer, Origen defends, as the fruit of Providence, the version of the LXX which accompanied the Church at its birth and in its first steps. "The eternal boundaries which your fathers set" (Prov 22:28) are none other than the Greek Scriptures (according to the LXX) venerated and transmitted in the Church for more than two centuries.

The one who makes this profession of faith in the LXX is precisely Origen, the author of the Hexapla, who promoted like nobody else in the Church the knowledge of the other Greek versions made by the Jews on the basis of the Hebrew Proto-Masoretic text. In the same letter to the African, Origen specifies that the whole of that enormous work had as its objective to become more familiar with the version of the LXX and its differences with the other translations "in order not to devalue the currency of the Churches that are under heaven and thus give, to those who seek it, occasion to slander public figures, as they wish, and to accuse those who are eminent in society."[23] This last would be a reference to the public discussions with the Jews in which Christians frequently came off looking foolish because their interlocutors denied that the passages quoted in the argumentation formed part of the Scriptures.

---

solitaire de Bethléem n'eut pas de peine à noyer sous ses sarcasmes les timides protestations de ce jeune africain traditionnaliste dont le crime impardonnable était d'ignorer l'hébreu" (Barthélemy, "Place de la Septante," 17).

22. Origen, *Ep. Afr.* 8.

23. Origen, *Ep. Afr.* 9. Barthélemy believes that the objective of the Hexapla went farther: it was a matter of enriching the Christian Bible with passages that were only found in the Bible of the Jews (cf. Barthélemy, "Place de la Septante," 15).

The Septuaginta Auctoritas: Lights

Irenaeus and Hilary on the Providential Translation of the LXX

This is not the place to introduce all the predecessors of Augustine in his defense of the authority of the LXX.[24] However, it is of interest to quote two more theologians who preceded him, one prior to Origen and the other subsequent, who expound with clarity the *providential* aspect of the Greek translation made in Alexandria.

Irenaeus (ca. 130–203) begins his argumentation with the new translations that the Jews have made of the OT, specifically those of "Theodotion of Ephesus and Aquila of Pontus." With them, the Jews "destroy the economy of God, as far as it is in their hands, and frustrate the testimony of the prophets, which God wrought."[25] In the view of the Asian author, there is a divine economy or providence which passes through the translation of the LXX, done long before the arrival of Christ, which was granted to the chosen people for the good of all peoples. The new translations would frustrate that divine providence.

The most interesting part of the argumentation of the bishop of Lyon is the parallelism that he establishes between the prodigious translation of the LXX interpreters in Alexandria, "on the basis of which God prepared and modeled beforehand our faith in his Son"[26] and the work of Ezra, who was inspired by God "to rewrite from memory all the words of the prior prophets and to restore to the people" the Scriptures that were destroyed when they were led into captivity in Babylon.[27] Both deeds belong to the same divine economy which preserves prophecy for the benefit of all nations. In addition, Egypt, the place where the Seventy Interpreters translated, again

---

24. A clear and synthetic presentation of these predecessors can be found in Veltri, "L'ispirazione della LXX."

25. "Tantam dispositionem Dei disolventes quantum ad ipsos est, frustrantes prophetarum testimonium quod operatus est Deus" (Irenaeus, *Haer.* 3.21.1; the Greek text is not preserved).

26. Irenaeus, *Haer.* 3.21.3.

27. Cf. Irenaeus, *Haer.* 3.21.2. Probably Irenaeus is basing himself on 4 Esd 14, where the Levite Ezra is described, in the Persian period, as receiving divine inspiration to again dictate the 24 books of the Scriptures which had been destroyed during the conquest of Jerusalem by the troops of Nebuchadnezzar ("Indeed, thy law has been burned, for which reason nobody knows the works that have been done by thee and those which are yet to be done. If I have found grace in thy sight, send me the Holy Spirit and I shall write all that which has been done in the world since the beginning, that which was written in thy law, so that men can find the path and those who should wish can live in the last days" [4 Esd 14:21–22]).

becomes a providential place in the history of salvation, as it was before, during the stay of the house of Jacob, and as it would be later, during the stay of Jesus with his parents fleeing from Herod.[28]

Hilary (ca. 315–367), for his part, showed himself to be really original when supporting the authority of the LXX. In his commentary on Psalm 2, the bishop of Poitiers took on the question of the differences between the Hebrew text and the Greek translation of the LXX.[29] By masterfully combining the rabbinic tradition about the existence of a double law, written and oral, and a statement of Jesus in the gospel of Matthew (Matt 23:2–3) which would seem to confirm it, he attributes the authority of the oral law to the Seventy Interpreters:

> Actually, in the intermediate times of the Law—before the Only Begotten Son of God, while remaining God the Word, became flesh—at the request of King Ptolemy, seventy elders translated the books of the Old Testament from Hebrew into Greek. Now even before that, Moses had established that in each synagogue there should be seventy doctors, because Moses himself, although he had put into writing the words of the Covenant, nevertheless in private had entrusted certain most secret mysteries of the arcane matters of the Law to seventy elders destined to be doctors thenceforth.
>
> The Lord, too, remembers their doctrine in the gospel, when he says: *The scribes and Pharisees have sat in the seat of Moses. Do all that they say, but do not do what they do.* Therefore, their teaching remains in the future: a teaching which has been accepted by the author of the Law himself and preserved by the same number and function of the elders.

In this way those elders translated these books and, after having acquired spiritual erudition in the arcane knowledge, in accordance with the Mosaic tradition, they translated from the Hebrew ambiguous expressions which had various meanings, by means of words with precise meanings and appropriate to the realities which they denote, moderating that plurality of sense in the texts with the erudition of their doctrine. Therefore it happens that later translators, with the diversity of their interpretations, have contributed a grave error to the pagans because, by being ignorant of this arcane tradition which has its origin in Moses, they have reproduced

---

28. Cf. Irenaeus, *Haer.* 3.21.3.
29. Hilary, *Trac. Ps. In Psalmum II.*

the ambiguous expressions of the Hebrew with an imprecision that is the product of their own opinions.[30]

The doctrine of the double legislation forms part of the rabbinic tradition. At Sinai Moses received not only the written law but also the oral law[31] which is transmitted from generation to generation[32] and which would wind up being put into writing in the Mishnah, first, and in the Talmud, later. The first link in that chain of transmission was supposed to be the seventy elders whom Moses chose in the desert (Num 11:16) and to whom he communicated that oral *traditio*. Jesus is supposed to have recognized that institution when he respected the authority of the "seat of Moses," who, having received the oral law, had authority to properly interpret the written law. Part of that chain of transmission of the interpretive key are the men of the great assembly or synagogue in the time of Ezra who played such an important role in the recovery of the Hebrew Scriptures, as Irenaeus reminds us.

In that same chain of tradition are supposed to be found the seventy elders of the synagogue charged with translating the written Law into Greek. In the version of the LXX, for the first time the conjunction of written law and oral law comes about. The former is necessarily ambiguous because as *letter* it needs to be interpreted. The authoritative interpretation lies with the seventy elders who received from Moses the "most secret mysteries of the arcane matters of the Law." The Greek translation or interpretation of the seventy elders is not a mere translation of an ambiguous letter from one language to another. It includes an interpretive *plus* which has the authority of the word revealed to Moses.

With this argumentation, Hilary causes the authority of the translation of the LXX to rest on the very Jewish tradition which argues for a double legislation, written and oral. That same doubling is what makes it possible for him to discredit the new Jewish translations into Greek (Aquila, Symmachus and Theodotion), which turn back to the ambiguous letter (Hebrew) by eliminating the interpretive *traditio* received from Moses himself and poured into the LXX.

---

30. Hilary, *Trac. Ps. In Psalmum II*, 2.

31. Cf. b. Ber. 5a.3.

32. "Moses received the Torah from Sinai and transmitted it to Joshua, Joshua to the elders, the elders to the prophets, the prophets transmitted it to the men of the Great Assembly. These said three things: be cautious in judgment, make many disciples, put a fence around the Torah" (m. 'Abot 1).

It is worthwhile to pause a moment to properly appreciate the value of Hilary's argument, which perhaps goes beyond what he himself might have intended. The bishop of Poitiers seems to be aware of the ambiguity of the Hebrew consonantal writing, as is proved by the example which he offers in the same commentary on Psalm 2: the different values of the first word of the Bible: "Beresith."[33] Actually, the Greek translation of the LXX represents the first moment in which a reading tradition of the Hebrew consonantal text becomes Scripture.[34] Until then the Scriptures as the word of God had to combine a written text, which was ambiguous because it was consonantal, and a reading tradition (which "inserted" the vowels in the act of reading). With the translation of the LXX the reading tradition rests on the letter itself and becomes one with it.

Hilary makes a point of emphasizing on more than one occasion that this process took place before the coming of Christ, for which reason the Christians cannot be accused of changing anything.[35] On the other hand, it is after the Incarnation that Pharisaic rabbinism puts its oral tradition into writing (first with the Mishnah, later with the Talmud) and when its particular reading tradition is joined with the consonantal text to become (around the seventh century C.E.) what we know as the Masoretic Text (supplied with vocalization, accentuation, and masora).

The OT "Ripened" in Alexandria

The review which I have conducted thus far has intended to catch, in the earliest Christian reflection, the idea of a divine providence as a foundation for the authority of the Greek version of the LXX. This review could well be synthesized with the apt expression which forms the title of an article by Barthélemy: "The Old Testament has ripened in Alexandria."[36] The Dominican scholar, on the basis of the sources from the early centuries, draws

---

33. Cf. Hilary, *Tr. Ps. In Psalmum II*, 2.

34. Cf. Carbajosa, "Vida de los manuscritos bíblicos."

35. In polemic with the new Greek translations done by the Jews, Hilary states: "But the authority of these seventy interpreters remains complete: first because they translated before the Incarnation of the Lord and they cannot be reproached for having used adulation when they were interpreting, since the period of the translation was so long prior" (Hilary, *Tr. Ps. In Psalmum II*, 3).

36. Barthélemy, "L'Ancien Testament a mûri."

his own conclusions about the value of the Septuagint for the Church today. It is worthwhile to go back over these conclusions in a summary form.[37]

If we speak of the OT of the Catholic Church we cannot put parentheses around what is happening in the Jewish community of Alexandria between the third and first centuries B.C.E. and turn to the "original" Hebrew text. Indeed, a canonical book like Wisdom was produced directly in Greek and in that community, and it plays a certain role in the Christian theology of the early centuries.[38] Other canonical books, which had a Hebrew original, have been preserved only in Greek due to the fact that they were translated and transmitted by the Jewish community of Alexandria.

The "ripening" of the OT, however, does not refer only to the parts of the Bible that are added to an originally shorter *corpus*. In Barthélemy's opinion, that ripening also happened within the books shared with the Jews ("protocanonical"), specifically in the many verses of the Greek translation which, while diverging from the Hebrew form, were received in the NT and fertilized Christian theology.[39] On the other hand, the Palestinian Pharisaism of the school of Hillel made an effort, in polemic with the Christians, "to definitively block the literary evolution of the Hebrew biblical text by taking as a point of reference an archaizing text established by learned men."[40]

In that effort intended to curb a literary (and theological) evolution, the rabbinate which was dominant in Palestine after the destruction of Jerusalem in the year 70 C.E. prepared itself to turn its back and disregard the Greek version with which the divine word had been incarnated in the great civilization conveyed by the Koine. What had been the Bible of the Alexandrian Jews was left in the hands of the Christians, thus putting an end to the "boldest attempt at *aggiornamento* ever undertaken by the synagogue."[41]

---

37. Barthélemy's reflections are expanded in another article which completes the first one: Barthélemy, "Place de la Septante."

38. The Latin Fathers, especially Ambrose (cf. *Spir.*, 1.10.117–18; 3.18.134–36; *Fid.*, 1.7.48–49; 4.11.143–44) and Augustine (cf. *Enarrat. Ps.*, 147.22; *Trin.* 4.20.27; *Tract. Ev. Jo.*, 20.13) turn to Wis 7:22–30 to refute the Arian heresy.

39. Barthélemy gives the example of the version of the LXX of Job 14:4 (*Who can be clean of all filth? No one, not even if his life on the earth lasts no more than a day*) widely quoted by the Greek and Latin fathers, which represents a *plus* in relation to the MT (*Who will take what is pure out of what is impure? No one!*) (Cf. Barthélemy, "L'Ancien Testament a muri," 360).

40. Barthélemy, "L'Ancien Testament a muri," 362.

41. Barthélemy, "L'Ancien Testament a muri," 363.

Of what did that *aggiornamento* consist? In Barthélemy's opinion, "the translation of the Scriptures into Greek Judaized the Koine more than it Hellenized Judaism. Thanks to it, words that until then had been profane and pagan became charged with typically Israelite resonances. From that time on, for the Jews of the diaspora, words of daily use ceased to be inappropriate with the message of Sinai: rather, they evoked it."[42] Let us think about the value that certain Greek words would acquire, with a marked weight on Hellene culture, in future Christian reflection and, even earlier, in the Jewish reflection of a book like Wisdom[43] or in authors like Philo of Alexandria or Flavius Josephus. *Logos, dikaiosyne, pneuma, Theos, doxa, aletheia, diatheke, arché* . . . are Greek terms that become loaded with a new meaning within the great framework of the Jewish Bible.[44]

This transfer "allowed the message of Israel to manifest itself in public in the heart of the Hellenistic civilization, in a language immediately understandable for the nations."[45] Following Irenaeus and Hippolytus, Barthélemy situates this *aggiornamento* in the same line as other updates of the Law: the Deuteronomistic one of Josiah in the seventh century B.C.E. and the one undertaken by Ezra in the fifth century B.C.E.[46]

Barthélemy concludes by claiming the LXX as the OT of the Church, even today: "If the Septuagint . . . is *the last updating* of the message of Moses in the face of the nations *before Pentecost*, it is the canonical and therefore original form of the Old Testament of the Pentecost people."[47]

I conclude this section with the words of Benedict XVI, in his academic lecture in Regensburg, which are especially lucid when understanding the value of the LXX:

---

42. Barthélemy, "L'Ancien Testament a muri," 366.

43. It suffices to see how terms that are very significant in Greek philosophy are used in this book, such as the verb λογίζομαι (2:1.21) or the nouns σοφία (chapters 6 to 9), ἀλήθεια (5:6), γνῶσις (7:17) or the expression μυστήρια Θεοῦ (2:22).

44. In this sense, the translation of the divine name revealed to Moses in Exod 3:14 as ἐγώ εἰμι ὁ ὤν is paradigmatic. Another clear example is the religious valence which the Greek verb ἐλπίζω acquires in the LXX (cf. Boyd-Taylor, "Semantics").

45. Barthélemy, "L'Ancien Testament a mûri," 368.

46. Barthélemy, "L'Ancien Testament a mûri," 368.

47. Barthélemy, "L'Ancien Testament a mûri," 370. In reaction to the tendency to turn, within the Church, to the Hebrew "original form" prior to its final update, the Dominican wonders: "Mais faut-il donc abandonner le fruit pour essayer de ressusciter à sa place la fleur en bouton qui l'a produit?" (Barthélemy, "L'Ancien Testament a muri," 370).

Biblical faith, during the Hellenistic era, met internally with the best of Greek thought, until it reached a reciprocal contact which afterward came out especially in the late sapiential literature. Today we know that the Greek translation of the Old Testament, done in Alexandria—the Bible of the "Seventy"—is more that a mere translation from the Hebrew text (which must perhaps be evaluated less than positively): it is in itself a textual witness, and a specific and important step in the history of Revelation, in which this encounter has come about which had a decisive significance for the birth of Christianity and its spread. At base, it is an encounter between faith and reason, between authentic enlightenment and religion.[48]

THE INSPIRATION OF THE SEVENTY INTERPRETERS

The third reason on which the authority of the version of the LXX rests, in the view of Augustine, is its inspired character. In his *De civitate Dei* he develops at length the conviction that the Seventy Interpreters were divinely inspired, something which he only mentions in passing in his correspondence with Jerome. In this argument, the bishop of Hippo is absolutely dependent on the *Letter of Aristeas*, although, as will be seen below, according to a version with late interpolations. When describing the translation done by the seventy-two elders sent from Jerusalem, Augustine states:

> It is told that there was in their words an agreement so remarkable, so astonishing and fully divine, having devoted themselves separately to this work (thus it pleased Ptolemy to test their fidelity), that none disagreed from another in any word that did not have the same meaning and the same value, or in the order of the words themselves; rather, as if it were a single translator, it was one single thing which all had interpreted; because, actually, the Spirit in all was only one. And they had received from God a remarkable gift, so that even with this the authority of those Scriptures was reinforced as being not human but, as they were in truth, divine, and thus that authority could be useful to the gentiles who, in the course of time, would come to believe in them, as we already see confirmed.[49]

---

48. Lecture of September 12, 2006, in *AAS* 98.10 (2006) 728–39 (732–33).
49. Augustine, *Civ.* 18.42.

Hebraica veritas versus Septuaginta auctoritatem

A version of the *Letter of Aristeas* had come down to Augustine in which the seventy-two elders are placed in seventy-two cells and work without contact on their respective translations, which then turn out to miraculously agree. This is an obvious sign of the Spirit who guided the work of translation, so that it must be held to be divinely authorized from then on. The Spirit who had guided the authors of the different books is the same one who was now guiding the translators. In this way the differences which the Greek text shows in relation to the Hebrew stay safe: they must be attributed to a divine power:

> Indeed, the Spirit which there was in the prophets when they wrote those things was the same one that existed also in the seventy men when they translated them. Well could that Spirit with divine authority have said another thing, as if that prophet had said both extremes, because both things were said by the same Spirit; and he could have said this same thing in another way, such that, if not the same words, then at least the same sense would appear to those who understood it well; as he could also have passed over something and added something; thus it would also be demonstrated by this that there was not in that work a human slavery which was subjecting the interpreter to the word, but rather a divine power which filled and ruled the mind of the interpreter.[50]

All the argumentation of the doctor from Hippo rests on a legend which, moreover, has been "enriched" over the course of time to highlight the inspiration of the LXX in its strongest sense. When I go on to identify the weaknesses of this argumentation I will work through this legend and the fragile foundations on which Augustine's reasons rest. In fact, the conviction that the Greek version had been inspired would be progressively abandoned after the holy doctor of the Church.

However, I cannot let pass, at this point, the debate which, in the fifties and sixties of the past century, again made the question of the inspiration of the LXX current. In this case, the reasons are no longer based on legends but on weighty theological arguments. Most of the authors who took part in this debate were French (or wrote in French), many of them Dominicans.[51] It was Pierre Benoit who took the initiative, again claiming

---

50. Augustine, *Civ.* 18.43.

51. Cf. Benoit, "Septante est-elle inspirée?"; Benoit, "L'inspiration des Septante"; Auvray, "Comment se pose le problème"; Grelot, "Sur l'inspiration"; Barthélemy, "L'Ancien Testament a mûri"; Dreyfus, "L'inspiration de la Septante"; Dubarle, "Note conjointe"; Barthélemy, "Place de la Septante." This debate has been summarized and taken up again

inspiration for the LXX, so unexpectedly that Barthélemy opened one of his articles with this statement: "Until the 5th century, the Old Testament coincided with the Septuagint for nine-tenths of the Church. From the 5th century to the year 1951 (the date of the article of Benoit in the *Festschrift für Max Meinertz*), the Septuagint has almost universally been considered in the Christian West to be a rather unfaithful translation in relation to which the Hebrew original must be preferred."[52] I will try to synthesize the reasons which led these modern authors to again propose the theological concept of inspiration for the Greek version. Specifically, I can reduce them to five.

The first reason is the one that Benoit puts forward in the article which opened the debate about the inspiration of the LXX. It has to do with the use which the authors of the NT make of the Greek version, in those passages in which it differs from the Hebrew text. In this case, "the inspired author of the NT approves and canonizes the novelty of thought" which he finds in the LXX.[53] Benoit himself anticipates a possible objection: in certain divergences of the LXX it was possible to recognize a human preparation providentially wanted by God which would find its confirmation in the inspired text of the NT; but those *pluses* of meaning would not be inspired in and of themselves.

The French Dominican replied that "the authors of the NT, when they quote the OT, in the form of the Septuagint, certainly claim to quote the Scriptures as such and they manifestly attribute to the Holy Spirit the thought that they are using."[54] If the hagiographers are aware of the difference which exists between the Greek text and the Hebrew in the passage quoted, then, when they use it, they receive the Greek text "as the authentic expression of divine thought."[55] In other words, the text quoted is, in its origin, inspired.

So are the LXX inspired only at some points? Paul Auvray attempts to head off this difficulty in the argumentation by reflecting on the nature of

---

later on by Italian authors: Buzzetti, "Traduzione della Bibbia"; Cimosa, "Traduzione greca"; Veltri, "L'ispirazione della LXX."

52. Barthélemy, "Place de la Septante," 13.

53. Benoit, "Septante est-elle inspirée?," 42. In this article, Benoit offers three examples of texts from the OT used in the NT according to the version of the LXX which differs from the MT: Ps 16:8–11 (LXX 15:8–11) quoted in Acts 2:25–31; Isa 7:14 quoted in Matt 1:23; Gen 12:3 and 22:18 quoted in Acts 3:25 and Gal 3:8–9.

54. Benoit, "Septante est-elle inspirée?," 48.

55. Benoit, "Septante est-elle inspirée?," 48.

the translators of the Greek version. As translators they do not need a special charism. If they are competent and the text they are translating is the original, the result will be the exact reproduction of an inspired text. In this sense the new work, faithful to the original, will be "mediately and equivalently inspired."[56] But if the translator inserts into the work a development of the thought, a particular interpretation or anything substantial, then he becomes an author. Then "he partakes of the charism of inspiration. He is no longer inspired as a translator; he is, occasionally, as an author."[57]

Pierre Grelot agrees with a different formulation. In his opinion it is necessary to recognize in the translator a *functional charism*, which includes the assistance of the Holy Spirit, directed toward translating well an inspired text. But in addition, when the translator becomes an author (because of a *plus* of meaning or a *plus* of text—whether fragments or an entire book), "the functional charism is completed with a scriptural charism, which he shares with all the other authors of the holy books, whether prophets, priests, singers, scribes, etc."[58]

The second reason has to do with those texts of the OT that belong to the Catholic canon and are not found in the Jewish (or Protestant) canon. These are necessarily inspired texts which only lately have received the name deuterocanonical. These texts have come down to us in Greek within the collection of books which constitutes the Septuagint. Sometimes they are additions (such as those in the book of Daniel or Esther). In other cases they are whole books which probably had a Hebrew original (such as 1 Maccabees, Baruch and certainly Sirach). Finally, there are books which were originally composed in Greek and are canonical (like Wisdom and 2 Maccabees).

In the case of these last texts, written originally in Greek, there can be no doubt that the charism of inspiration can and should be attributed to their authors. Going further, Grelot wonders whether for the rest of the "additions" in the LXX with a hypothetical Hebrew original it is sufficient to speak of a "juridically authentic" version (the fidelity to the original of which is in fact unverifiable) or if it is possible to say more. In his opinion, "it is better to think that these Greek texts, *as such*, are canonical and

---

56. Auvray, "Comment se pose le problème," 333.
57. Auvray, "Comment se pose le problème," 333–34.
58. Grelot, "Sur l'inspiration," 413.

inspired, without prejudice to the intrinsic value that their Hebrew originals possess."[59]

The third reason has to do with the practically unanimous opinion of the Greek and Latin Fathers until the fifth century that the Greek version of the LXX was inspired. Several of the authors who took part in this recent debate offered a review of the earliest Christian theologians and their statements about the Alexandrian version.[60] If these authors based themselves on tradition it was because the arguments of early Christian reflection obviously go beyond the testimony of the *Letter of Aristeas*.

The fourth reason to argue for the inspiration of the LXX is closely linked to what was discussed above about the providential aspect of this translation, which was considered *praeparatio evangelica*. Now they were going farther: Does providential character imply the charism of inspiration? Bearing in mind that "the transition from Hebrew to Greek was a capital enterprise intended to open the treasure of the Scriptures to the pagan world," Benoit wonders whether perhaps "God has not inspired these changes in view of the pagan readers."[61]

Grelot, along the same lines, speaks of a "progress of revelation in the Septuagint."[62] In his view, the translation of the LXX probably marks "an advance within revelation itself." Even so, Grelot closely links that progress or advance in revelation to its reception because of the Christ event attested in the NT, an inspired text, and in subsequent ecclesiastical tradition, and thus he returns to the first reason that was studied above.

The fifth and final reason has to do with the very concept of inspiration. In Benoit's opinion, resistance to attributing that charism to some translators comes from an excessively narrow understanding of the concept of inspiration, like the one apparently held by Jerome, who distinguished between "prophets" (authors of the Hebrew books, and therefore inspired) and mere "translators" (the Seventy Interpreters). Thus inspiration and revelation are identified. But the work of the Holy Spirit is richer and more dynamic, as attested by John Chrysostom, who states that it was that same Holy Spirit which "'inspired' Moses to compose the Scriptures, just as he

---

59. Grelot, "Sur l'inspiration," 410.

60. Cf., especially, Auvray, "Comment se pose le problème"; Benoit, "L'inspiration des Septante"; Veltri, "L'ispirazione della LXX."

61. Benoit, "L'inspiration des Septante," 174–75.

62. Grelot, "Sur l'inspiration," 407.

Hebraica veritas versus Septuaginta auctoritatem

'inspired' Ezra to restore them, 'sent' the prophets and, lastly, 'predisposed' the Seventy to translate."[63]

On this basis, Benoit thinks that it is possible to distinguish, in the very work of the LXX, between inspiration and revelation. By inspiration we understand "that impulse which sparked and carried out the transposition of the biblical message into Greek thought," while revelation would include "all the new truths which the translators received before or during their work and taught in the name of God through their work."[64]

---

63. Benoit, "L'inspiration des Septante," 177. The statement of John Chrysostom is found in *Hom. Hebr.* 8.4.

64. Benoit, "L'inspiration des Septante," 177.

CHAPTER 6

The *Septuaginta Auctoritas*
Shadows

AFTER EXPOUNDING AT LENGTH the reasons in favor of the authority of the LXX, with all the validity they may have, I will now turn to the weak points present in the development of those reasons.

ECCLESIASTICAL PLURALITY, TEXTUAL PLURALITY

First, it is necessary to carefully examine the two statements on which the first reason in favor of the authority of the LXX is based: the Septuagint is the Bible of the Christians and the Bible of the apostles.

The statement that the LXX is the Bible of the Christians or of the Church enjoys a certain amount of popularity, such that in recent decades it has been repeated as much in the academic sphere as in informational contexts without need for any special justification.[1] I will begin with the fact that such a statement has a basis *in re*, as has previously been seen. It should be borne in mind that Christianity spread at a time when Koine Greek was the lingua franca of the empire, so that the translation of the LXX which was circulating through the synagogues of the Mediterranean constituted the Scriptures of the Christians who were being converted from Hellenistic Judaism or were coming to the faith from the gentile world.

---

1. Cf. Law, *When God Spoke Greek*; Fernández Marcos, *Septuaginta*; Wagner, "Septuagint"; Hengel, *Septuagint as Christian Scripture*; Müller, *First Bible of the Church*.

Hebraica veritas versus Septuaginta auctoritatem

Nevertheless, a statement that claims exclusivity for the Greek version (including the *Vetus Latina* version which is based on it) must come up against the fact that the Septuagint (in the first four centuries of Christianity) was not *the* Bible of the *whole* Church. Barthélemy's statement, included above, "Until the 5th century, the Old Testament coincided with the Septuagint for nine-tenths of the Church," speaks, beyond the greater or lesser precision of the statistical fact, of a small percentage of Christians who approached the OT through a version that was not the Alexandrian one.[2]

Indeed, the Syriac church, spread over a strip of territory which included the north of present-day Syria and Iraq, the south of Turkey, and the northwest of Iran, from the beginning used a Syriac translation of the OT made from a Hebrew Proto-Masoretic text toward the middle of the second century C.E. and known as the Peshitta.[3] In all likelihood, the Syriac church followed the same pattern as the Greek churches: it inherited the Scriptures (OT) already translated into their language by the Jews. In fact, it seems that most of the books of the Peshitta were translated by the Jews, although in time the synagogue must have abandoned this version, such that the whole textual tradition that has come down to us is Christian.[4]

It is true that theology in Syriac did not flower until the end of the third and the beginning of the fourth centuries C.E., in the hands of Aphrahat and Ephrem, who used the Peshitta, but even by the end of the second century and the beginning of the third century Christian literature in Syriac is attested[5] which could be using that version.[6] Paraphrasing a particular expression of the great scholar of Syriac literature, Sebastian Brock, it is

---

2. Timothy M. Law also qualifies his statement that "it was the first time in Christian history that a Bible other than or not based on the Septuagint was promoted for use in the church" by adding: "Outside of a small population of Christians who had been using the Syriac Peshitta based on the Hebrew Bible" (Law, *When God Spoke Greek*, 161).

3. Cf. Drijvers, "Syrian Christianity."

4. To learn the essential data about the Syriac version, cf. Carbajosa, "Peshitta."

5. Specifically the work of Bardaisan, *Book of the Laws of Countries* (cf. Drijvers, *Book of the Laws*) and the *Diatessaron* of Tatian (although this has not come down to us in Syriac) (Cf. Petersen, *Tatian's Diatessaron*).

6. Adalbert Merx argues that Bardaisan quotes the Peshitta when he comments on Psalm 8 (cf. Merx, *Bardesanes von Edessa*, 19). It is harder to discern what was the source of the OT quotations in Tatian's Diatessaron, since the work has not been preserved in Syriac and there are few fragments in Greek, although there are authors who believe that he could have used the Peshitta (cf. Joosten, "Old Testament Quotations"; Shedinger, "Did Tatian Use?").

necessary for the Church to recognize "a third lung" beyond the two with which it consciously breathes, which represent the Western (Latin) Church and the Eastern (Greek) Church.[7]

The proof that this Church, and the theological literature which it produced, did not depend on the Greek version of the LXX, is that it did not take long to come into conflict with the way of quoting the OT (according to the LXX) of the Greek theological literature of the neighboring Antiochian Church. Indeed, the Syriac church was characterized from early on by a rich cultural (and commercial) relationship with the Greek world of Antioch, to the point that even today many Greek works translated into Syriac and vice versa are preserved.[8] It was natural that, in the process of translating the Greek authors, the Syriac interpreters would realize that the text of the OT that was quoted (the LXX) diverged from the form that they knew (the Peshitta). The prestige of the Greek theologians, and the influence of their theology, caused non-original *lectiones*, coming from the LXX, to start to enter the textual tradition of the Peshitta[9] and even for a new Syriac translation from the Greek to be done (the Syro-Hexapla, beginning of the seventh century); this, however, did not manage to displace the Peshitta.

Augustine's statement, quoted above, "the Churches of Christ think that no one should place himself ahead of the authority of these men" (the Seventy Interpreters), must, therefore, be trimmed back. Certainly it could not be said of all the churches of Christ and even less in the fifth century, when the bishop of Hippo was writing.

The second statement that must be revised is the one that presents the LXX as "the Bible of the apostles," the one which, according to Augustine, *was used* by those who followed Jesus and later composed the books of the NT. I have had occasion to reveal the lack of foundation of the contrary thesis, held by Jerome, which stated that the apostles quoted the Scriptures according to the Hebrew (Proto-Masoretic) text. A superficial study of the quotations from the OT in the NT is enough to make one realize that many of them come from the version of the LXX when it departs from the MT. Now the time has come to clarify how far it is possible to defend the statement that the LXX is the Bible of the authors of the NT.

---

7. Cf. Brock, "Syriac Orient." Cf. my reflections about this matter in Carbajosa, "A los 500 años," 30–32.

8. Cf. Drijvers, "Syrian Christianity"; Brock, "Greek into Syriac."

9. Cf. Carbajosa, "Syriac Old Testament Tradition."

In order to shed light on this matter it is necessary to start with a serious textual study of the quotations from the OT in the NT, as I pointed out when criticizing Jerome's thesis that the apostles quoted the Scriptures according to the Hebrew text. Fortunately, this field has developed a great deal in recent decades, thanks to greater knowledge of the sources of the OT available in the first century C.E.,[10] and to advances in the textual criticism of the NT and its way of quoting the Scriptures.[11]

One of the conclusions which recent studies have reached is that it is necessary to abandon the idea that the authors of the NT had a single alternative available: either to quote from a Hebrew text of the Proto-Masoretic type or to quote according to the Greek version which we know as the Septuagint. Today it is known that in the first century C.E. Hebrew texts were circulating which were not from the Proto-Masoretic or Pre-Masoretic family. In the same way, the Greek text of the OT available at that time was not only the one of the "pure" LXX form. In fact, a good number of quotations from the OT in the NT seem to have come from Greek textual forms which differed from the LXX and which have not come down to us, whether because they reflected genuine readings of the Septuagint that have been lost, or because they attest early forms of correcting the first Greek version on the basis of Hebrew manuscripts, forms which we are only now beginning to learn about.[12]

Now is the time to go back to the discussion about the quotation of Isa 7:14 that is found in Matt 1:22–23. This study can turn out to be paradigmatic, since it constitutes one of the classic examples to show how the NT uses the Greek version of the LXX; and yet, as was seen earlier, it was

---

10. Cf. *THB* 1A.

11. Karrer calls attention to two dynamics which determine the way of quoting and the text which is quoted. The first is the weight of oral tradition in the knowledge of the Scriptures which are quoted, such that some differences with the manuscripts of the LXX available today could be attributed to an "oral development" of the text. The second may explain the plurality of textual sources of which a single NT author makes use. Specifically, Paul would find himself obliged to quote based on the manuscripts that he found in the different communities through which he passed on his voyages (cf. Karrer, "Septuagint Text," 614–18).

12. John 19:37 quotes Zech 12:10 according to a Greek version which is not the LXX and which could be the early revision of the LXX that is found in papyrus 8ḤevXIIgr, from the caves of *Naḥal Ḥever*. Zech 12:10 is not preserved in that scroll, but the coincidences of that revision, and of the same passage in Zechariah, with that of Theodotion which is preserved, make the hypothesis more than plausible (cf. Bynum, *Fourth Gospel*). Cf. Hanhart, "Bedeutung der Septuaginta," 400–409; Barthélemy, *Devanciers d'Aquila*.

used by Jerome to conclude the contrary: that Matthew used the Hebrew text. The study will help us to understand the Dalmatian's reasons and will show us that the Greek text available to the evangelist did not coincide, as such, with the one attested by the LXX.[13] I will begin by presenting the text of Matthew and the Hebrew and Greek sources:

> Matt 1:23: ἰδοὺ ἡ <u>παρθένος</u> ἐν γαστρὶ <u>ἕξει</u> καὶ τέξεται υἱόν, καὶ <u>καλέσουσιν</u> τὸ ὄνομα αὐτοῦ Ἐμμανουήλ, "Behold, the virgin shall be pregnant and shall give birth to a son and they shall call his name Emmanuel."

> LXX[B]: ἰδοὺ ἡ παρθένος ἐν γαστρὶ λη(μ)ψεται καὶ τέξεται υἱόν[14], καὶ καλέσεις τὸ ὄνομα αὐτοῦ Εμμανουηλ, "Behold, the virgin shall conceive and shall give birth to a son and you shall call his name Emmanuel."

> MT: הִנֵּה הָעַלְמָה הָרָה וְיֹלֶדֶת בֵּן וְקָרָאת שְׁמוֹ עִמָּנוּ אֵל, "Behold, the damsel is pregnant and gives birth to a son and you shall call his name Emmanuel."

The three terms in Matthew's quotation that turn out to be keys to finding out the textual source from which it is derived are the noun παρθένος and the verbs ἕξει and καλέσουσιν. We have already seen how Jerome tiptoed around the noun παρθένος, "virgin," taking for granted that it was a valid translation of the Hebrew עלמה, "young damsel." Actually, there is no doubt that the author of the gospel had before him a Greek text with the term παρθένος, which is just the reading found in the LXX, for otherwise he would have translated the Hebrew עלמה as Aquila, Symmachus, and Theodotion do: νεανις, "young damsel." The fact that the verbs in the first line of the gospel text are in the future (ἕξει καὶ τέξεται) also shows that the quotation has been taken from a Greek text similar to that of the LXX and not from the Hebrew.

However, Jerome is right when he calls attention to the difference between the expression of Matthew ἐν γαστρὶ ἕξει and that of the LXX, ἐν

---

13. In this study, I follow Menken, "Textual Form."

14. The *Codex Vaticanus* and the *Siri Rescriptus* read ἐν γαστρὶ λη(μ)ψεται while the *Sinaiticus* and *Alexandrinus* attest ἐν γαστρὶ ἕξει. The first reading is the *lectio difficilior* while the second appears to have entered into the manuscript tradition because of the influence of Matt 1:23. *Pace* Rahlfs and Ziegler, who consider the second reading original (cf. Menken, "Textual Form," 150).

γαστρὶ λη(μ)ψεται and the difference between καλέσουσιν (Matt 1:23) and καλέσεις (LXX Isa 7:14):

> If we set out to argue about words, "she shall have" is not the same as "she shall conceive" nor "they shall call" as "you shall call."[15]

Normally the differences between the version of the LXX and the text quoted by Matthew are explained as adjustments by the evangelist to fit the passage OT to its context. There is, however, a simpler explanation. The evangelist might have had before him a version of the LXX corrected according to a Hebrew text. In that version he would have found the expression ἐν γαστρὶ ἕξει, which, in fact, is a better translation of the Hebrew הרה. In that same manuscript there would also appear the form καλέσουσιν, which could attest to a Hebrew variant וקרא ("and he shall call," instead of MT וקראת, "and you shall call") like the one found in 1QIs^a.[16]

This example shows how the question of the textual source of the quotations from the OT in the NT is more complex that what may outwardly seem to be a choice between the Hebrew text and the Greek of the LXX. The two statements in question, which claim to present, respectively, the Hebrew Proto-Masoretic text and the version of the LXX as *the* Bible of the apostles, do not respect the fact that the authors of the NT in some cases quote from the Hebrew text and in many others do so from the Greek of the LXX. But there are yet others in which the Greek text quoted corresponds to a revision of the Septuagint.

WHICH LXX ARE WE TALKING ABOUT?

The textual complexity of the Greek text of the OT which the authors of the NT used now leads to the criticism that must be directed at the second argument in favor of the authority of the LXX: its providential role in the birth of Christianity. Indeed, it was previously possible to recognize that a certain amount of development in early Christian theology, attested in the NT, is based on an expressive form of the LXX which departs from the

---

15. Jerome, *Letter* 57.8 (*Epistolary*, I, 554).

16. Menken anticipates the question of why this revised version of the LXX does not correct παρθένος to νεᾶνις: "... the evidence presented above shows that νεᾶνις was not a standard translation of עלמה. Besides, the translation by παρθένος became problematic only when Christians appealed to Isa 7:14 to support their view of Jesus as born from a virgin. Before that moment, this translation did not need to present theological difficulties to a Jewish reader" (Menken, "Textual Form," 154).

Hebrew text. That is not the fact that I wish to criticize. The statement of the providential role of the LXX becomes problematic when one wants to make of the Greek version a coherent and closed whole which must be accepted as a decisive step toward the crowning point of the revelation achieved in Jesus Christ.

Nothing could be farther from reality than this image of the LXX as a coherent and closed whole. This image is closely linked in our heads to the format of the codex, which is capable of containing in one volume a particular number of books, forming a complete whole. We should remember, though, that this publishing format, as opposed to the scroll, began to become dominant starting in the third–fourth centuries C.E. and especially in Christian circles.[17] The editions of the LXX with which we are familiar today, which determine our understanding of that version, are based (both in the number of books and in the text) on the great codices of the fourth century (*Vaticanus* and *Sinaiticus*) and fifth century C.E. (*Alexandrinus* and *Ephraemi Syri Rescriptus*), which are the work of Christians.[18] It is incorrect to say that those editions available to us present, as such, *the* Greek text of the different books that were translated (or composed) originally in Alexandria between the end of the third century and end of the first century B.C.E.

To what textual reality are we referring when we speak of the Greek version of the LXX? Are we sure that we are speaking of the same text that the authors of the NT had in front of them (if indeed they had the same Greek texts available among themselves)? Are we sure that we are familiar with the Greek texts of the OT that Christian theologians of the second century C.E. like Justin and Irenaeus had available to them?

The books translated into Greek originally circulated in scrolls and, in time, they began to be copied for use in the synagogues scattered along the shores of the Mediterranean. We know that some of these scrolls were

---

17. Cf. Nongbri, *God's Library*; Hurtado, *Earliest Christians Artifacts*; Bagnall, *Early Christian Books*; Gamble, *Books and Readers*; Roberts and Skeat, *Birth of the Codex*; Blanchard, *Débuts du codex*.

18. The Cambridge edition, which only covers the Pentateuch and the historical books, reproduces the text of the *Codex Vaticanus*, with a very rich critical apparatus: Brooke et al., *Old Testament in Greek*. The *editio minor* of Göttingen presents an eclectic text which, however, rests on the choices of the codices *Vaticanus* and *Sinaiticus*: Rahlfs and Hanhart, *Septuaginta*. The *editio maior*, which is about to be completed, is already taking into account, in the creation of the eclectic text, a large quantity of manuscripts, although the great codices continue to have a decisive weight, both in textual choices and in the number of books: *Septuaginta: Vetus Testamentum Graecum*.

corrected in order to bring the text of the LXX closer to the Hebrew of the Pre-Masoretic type. We also know that some of these scrolls were replaced by others which contained new translations, as is the case with the book of Daniel, the ecclesiastical version of which is identified with the version of Theodotion and not with the original of the LXX.

The different scrolls began to constitute a coherent whole in the Christian editions which are found in the earliest codices. But these codices differ among themselves both in the number of books (canon) and in the textual form of the same (text). Moreover, in those editions a text is included which can be called *ecclesiastical*, which in some books was corrected, after the NT era, in relation to its original form. A clear example is the Greek text of Job that is found in the earliest complete (Christian) codices of the Greek Bible, *Sinaiticus* and *Vaticanus*, which incorporates many verses that the original version had failed to translate.

But beyond the textual complexity which makes a statement like "the first Christians used the Greek Bible of the LXX" problematic, other aporias are found when one wants to attribute a providential value to the whole version. There is no doubt that, in the view of the Christians, certain developments of thought or theology which the Jewish community of Alexandria introduced in the act of translating the LXX were providential. As Irenaeus and Hilary had already said, they must be understood as being in the same line of the progress of the text that took place in the time of Josiah and the time of Ezra. The relevant question is whether that progress should be attributed, as a whole, to all of the original translation of the LXX or whether, on the contrary, we are obliged to give a "canonical" embrace to those parts in which progress accepted by the NT or by early Christian reflection can be identified.

If one opts to consider the totality of the text of the Greek version of the LXX canonical (beyond the set of textual problems which the very concept of "LXX" entails), and, therefore, self-sufficient in its relationship with the Hebrew text (because it is an authentic, providential or inspired version, as one chooses), some serious problems are encountered. It will suffice to list four.

First, we would have to ponder what the value is of the "second" edition of the text of Jeremiah, which was developed before Christ and which we have received through the Proto-Masoretic text (and in Qumran). Let us not forget that the long text is considered canonical by the Catholic Church. A second problem has to do with the quotations of the OT in the

NT which come from a Hebrew text when it differs from the version of the LXX. Let us think about the fulfillment quotations in Matthew. We are talking about an expressive form accepted by the NT which is not found in the LXX.

A third problem, connected to the preceding one, has to do with those passages in which the hermeneutical development of the translation of the LXX diverges from the Palestinian Jewish tradition in Hebrew. There are cases in which Christian theology feels more comfortable starting with the second tradition, as happens with the identification of the Messiah with the servant of Yahweh in Isa 42:1. The version of the LXX, in that passage, identifies the servant with Israel:[19]

> MT (=1QIsᵃ): Behold, my servant whom I uphold, my chosen one with whom my soul is pleased.

> LXX: Jacob is my servant, I will help him, Israel is my chosen one, my soul accepts him.

Finally, the affirmation of the version of the LXX as a coherent and closed whole, of a providential (or inspired) nature, makes the understanding of the translation itself difficult. Indeed, we cannot forget that the LXX is a translation of a Hebrew text. Moreover, unlike modern translations, in many cases the Greek version reproduces and does not resolve the ambiguity of the original text. In this regard, many passages of the LXX are clarified by turning to the Hebrew text—obviously, when the two coincide.

CAN INSPIRATION BE ATTRIBUTED TO A TRANSLATOR?

The Argument of the *Letter of Aristeas*

The last reason on which Augustine based his support for the authority of the LXX was its inspired nature, which he deduced from the tradition received from the *Letter of Aristeas*. The criticism of this argument involves

---

19. Cf. Gzella, "New Ways in Textual Criticism"; Kooij, "Servant of the Lord." Not so in other passages, in which, on the contrary, the Greek version of the LXX adds a *plus* to the sense which identifies the servant with the figure of the Messiah, as happens in Isa 53:2. Indeed, when translating the Hebrew noun יוֹנֵק, "tender shoot," as παιδίον, "child," the LXX refers to Isa 9:5, where the Messiah is described and announced: "because a child [παιδίον] has been born to us, a son [υἱός] has been given to us."

two stages. In the first one I will show how in the original version of that letter there is no trace of the miraculous nature of the translation. In the second stage I will critically examine the arguments in favor of the inspiration of the LXX which arose in the second half of the twentieth century.

The first task is relatively simple. Augustine unhesitatingly accepted an account from what is known as the *Letter of Aristeas* in which the seventy-two elders were placed in seventy-two cells and in seventy-two days independently translated the whole Hebrew Torah into Greek, with the result that all the versions agreed. It was a miraculous event which, obviously, resulted from divine will (and inspiration). This miraculous aspect, however, did not belong to the original version of the Letter. On the contrary, the Letter says that Demetrius, the director of the royal library of Alexandria, gathered the seventy-two

> in a house which had been duly furnished near the shore—a magnificent building in a very quiet situation—and invited the men to carry out the work of translation, all that they would require being handsomely provided. They set to completing their several tasks, reaching agreement among themselves on each by comparing versions. The result of their agreement thus was made into a fair copy by Demetrius. The business of their meeting occupied them until the ninth hour. . . . At the first hour of the day they attended the court daily, and after offering salutation to the king, retired to their own quarters. Following the custom all the Jews, they washed their hands in the sea in the course of their prayers to God, and then proceeded to the reading and explication of each point.[20]

As is seen, the letter presents the seventy-two in a situation of shared work, comparing opinions. There is no trace of *inspiration* in this account. The only element which may refer to any divine intervention is the fact that the translation was completed in seventy-two days, a piece of information that belongs to the original version of the letter. For good reason, the author of the letter has the intention of arguing that the shared work of the seventy-two elders was not untouched by the hand of God and should be preferred to the other translations or revisions of the LXX that were probably beginning in his time.

What is the source of the details of the seventy-two cells and the final agreement of the seventy-two versions prepared independently? These details belong to an independent tradition originally attested by the

---

20. *Let. Aris.* 301–5.

anonymous work *Exhortatio ad Graecos*,[21] by Irenaeus[22] and by a *baraita* of the Babylonian Talmud.[23] Both in this late tradition and in the work *De vita Mosis* by Philo of Alexandria (ca. 15 B.C.E.–41 C.E.),[24] one detects the will to explain the inspired nature of the Greek translation, perhaps in an apologetic context that is more marked than the one which the *Letter of Aristeas* itself has.

Probably the most legendary details of the *Letter of Aristeas*, attested beginning in the second century C.E., could have developed as a fanciful account connected with the visit to the island of Pharos, perhaps on the occasion of the annual pilgrimages to celebrate the Greek translation of the Law,[25] which Philo said he was familiar with in his time.[26] In conclusion, the affirmation of the inspiration of the LXX cannot be based on late, legendary accounts created precisely to support what was to be proved.

Is It Possible to Defend the Inspiration of the LXX Today?

The defense of the inspiration of the LXX has by no means always been based on the legend of Aristeas. Now is the time to critically evaluate the arguments of the authors who in the fifties and sixties of the twentieth century tried to reclaim the inspired nature of the Greek version. Some of the authors who took part in that discussion took on the role of devil's advocate by presenting objections to the thesis that was being defended.[27] I will start with those objections and subsequently add others of my own.

---

21. *Exhort. Grae.*, cap. 13 (second–third century C.E.).

22. Irenaeus, *Haer.* 3.21.2.

23. B. Meg. 9a (probably from the first half of the second century C.E.). A careful study of this expansion of the *Letter of Aristeas* in the rabbinic literature is found in Wasserstein and Wasserstein, *Legend of the Septuagint*, 51–83.

24. In *Mos.* 2.37, Philo adds new details to the account of the translation (among them that it was done on the island of Pharos, a detail which it shares with the *Exhort. Grae.*) and goes so far as to make explicit the Greek term which indicates divine inspiration: ἐνθουσιῶντες.

25. Cf. Barthélemy, "Pourquoi la Torah," 27.

26. Philo, *Mos.* 2.41–44.

27. Especially Dreyfus, "L'inspiration de la Septante," and Dubarle, "Note conjointe." In addition, Grelot, "Sur l'inspiration," 402–5, proceeds in his article by following the method of scholasticism, first presenting the objections to the thesis of the inspiration of the LXX (*Videtur quod non*).

Grelot presents three objections to the inspiration thesis which he himself defends. The first objection has already been considered: the legendary nature of the *Letter of Aristeas*, which constitutes the basis on which many Greek and Latin fathers place their statement that the Seventy Interpreters were inspired. The second objection is focused on the errors of the Greek translation. It is hard to speak of an inspired version when we can identify numerous translation errors. For good reason, *inerrancy*, however it may be understood, must go along with an inspired text.[28] Grelot gives as an example the original Greek version of Daniel, a translation "so bad that, following Origen, the early Septuagint was replaced by the version of Theodotion."[29] The third and final objection is based on the uselessness of the very hypothesis that it is wished to defend: it is not necessary to attribute to the translators a charism that is peculiar to the prophets and apostles. It is enough to speak of a functional charism which the Holy Spirit grants them to carry out their task.

Dreyfus, for his part, also presents three objections. The first has to do with the ecclesiastical text of Daniel which in the LXX agrees with the version of Theodotion. What does it mean to attribute the charism of inspiration to one whom Jerome called "a blasphemous Jew born after the passion of Christ"?[30] How can a text be considered inspired if it originates in dialectic with the NT reading of it?[31]

The second objection is closely connected to the first one, but it goes a step farther. Indeed, the version of the LXX of Daniel was abandoned and replaced by that of Theodotion. But there are cases in which the only Greek translation that exists of the canonical book, the one which therefore came into the ecclesiastical Septuagint, seems to be the work of Jewish rabbis

---

28. Grelot's text was prior to the promulgation of the dogmatic Constitution *Dei Verbum*, from the Second Vatican Council, which abandoned a certain "rigid" understanding of *inerrancy* to speak of *truth for our salvation* (cf. *Dei Verbum* 11: "the books of Scripture must be acknowledged as teaching solidly, faithfully and without error that truth which God wanted put into sacred writings for the sake of salvation").

29. Grelot, "Sur l'inspiration," 403.

30. Jerome, *Letter* 112.19 (*Epistolary*, II, 308).

31. Actually, Dreyfus was already aware of the complexity implied by the attribution to "Theodotion" of the translation of the book of Daniel, including the possibility of a pre-Christian, proto-Theodotion and a second "Theodotion" who is no more than a mere reviser. However, Dreyfus' objection makes sense considering that the Christian theologians of the third and fourth centuries who argued for the inspiration of the LXX thought that Theodotion was a Jew who had corrected the Greek OT in polemic with Christianity.

who were already living in the Christian era (first and second centuries C.E.). Basing himself on the studies of Barthélemy,[32] Dreyfus calls attention to the fact that the Greek version of Ecclesiastes which is read in the LXX seems to be the work of Aquila (a disciple of Rabbi Akiva, second century C.E.), while the Greek translations, which are considered "ecclesiastical," of Lamentations, Songs and Ruth must be attributed to Theodotion.[33] Plainly, attributing the charism of inspiration to rabbinic translations or revisions in the Christian era turns out to be problematic.

The third and final objection has to do with the non-canonical third book of Ezra, which appears in the textual tradition of the LXX as Ezra A. Recognizing the inspiration of the LXX as a whole would imply recognizing the inspiration, and therefore the canonicity, of a book which does not appear on the lists of the Councils of Florence or Trent.

Other Aporias

I will now complete these objections with a couple of reflections which strike me as relevant and which should be borne in mind in this debate. The first has to do with a problem which modern versions of the OT have had to face in recent decades. It is an aporia which I mentioned previously and to which I will now return because the question of inspiration is involved. Before the discoveries of the manuscripts of the Dead Sea, the so-called deuterocanonical books were translated into our modern languages from Greek, the only language in which they were preserved.[34] In fact, they were translated from the Greek as if it were the original language and, in a certain way, as if they were inspired versions. But the appearance of new Hebrew fragments of book of Sirach (today about three-quarters of the "original" has been recovered), as well as the Aramaic and Hebrew of the book of Tobit, pose two intrinsically connected questions: Which is the inspired text? What text should be translated in our modern versions?

---

32. Barthélemy, *Devanciers d'Aquila*.

33. In Barthélemy's opinion, "Theodotion" was probably Jonathan ben Uzziel, a disciple of Hillel and a contemporary of Saint Paul.

34. The Hebrew fragments of the book of Sirach found in the Geniza of the synagogue of Cairo at the end of the nineteenth century had not yet brought up the problem of the source from which to translate, perhaps because of their fragmentary character and because little was yet known about the relationship between the Hebrew text and the Greek.

Hebraica veritas versus Septuaginta auctoritatem

The solution adopted by some authors favorable to the inspiration of the LXX, namely, to consider the texts or fragments which have come down to us only in Greek as canonical and inspired,[35] is problematic. If the Hebrew originals discovered or those which may come to light in the future, showed that the Greek editions contain errors of translation or simply that they attest secondary variant *lectiones* (in their Hebrew *Vorlagen*), it would be hard to continue to argue for the inspiration of these versions. As was previously seen, in the case of the Hebrew and Aramaic fragments of Sirach and Tobit which have been discovered, the relationship between the original text and the ancient versions is not at all clear, for which reason this problem can only be posed but not, at present, resolved.

The second reflection has to do with the very concept of inspiration. It was previously seen how Benoit looked into this matter to try to overcome the objections which arose from attributing that charism to a translation. The chief objection, however, remains. *Inspiration* has to do with a very specific motion of the Holy Spirit oriented toward the production of a text which has a unique status in the life of the Church as a written testimony of revelation. *Inspiration* speaks of the truth for our salvation of what is contained in some books, written *ex profeso* by the initiative of the Holy Spirit.

---

35. This is the case of Grelot, who, when speaking of those texts, states that "it is better to think that these Greek texts, *as such*, are canonical and inspired, without prejudice to the intrinsic value that their Hebrew originals possess" (Grelot, "Sur l'inspiration," 398. 410). In addition, the *Jerusalem Bible* (French first edition, 1961; English version, first edition, 1966) states in its introduction to the book of Sirach that "The Church recognises the canonicity only of the Greek text and from this our translation is made," although no justification is given for such a sweeping statement. Curiously, the *editio typica* of the Neo-Vulgate, on which our liturgical translations later than the eighties are based (the *editio typica altera* is from 1986), poses for itself, in its *Praenotanda*, the textual problem of the book (two Greek editions, one Hebrew and one Syriac) and asks itself from which text to start. Since at the current state of research it is impossible to understand the relationship between the different editions with a view to identifying a "primitive" text, the Neo-Vulgate is based on the classical Latin text (which came from the *Vetus*, since Jerome did not translate it), which is corrected (or completed) by the Greek, Hebrew and Syriac editions, when the multiple attestation makes this advisable. The statement which I mentioned from the *Jerusalem Bible* disappears starting with the third edition of the original French edition (1998), and is replaced by new introductions to the book of Sirach in every version. The third Spanish edition says: "Given the fragmentary state of the Hebrew text, our translation has been made from the Greek text (more precisely, from the three principal manuscripts, Sinaiticus, Alexandrinus and Vaticanus, which form what is called the 'received text'), while indicating in notes particular variants of the Hebrew."

We can proclaim "Word of God" when we finish the liturgical reading in a modern version, and this is right because what comes to us in translation is inspired content. However, to say that some particular translators, in their complete work, have been *inspired*, is enormously problematic if we want to maintain the specific content of that charism and not dissolve it by confusing it with the diverse and rich motions of the Holy Spirit in the life of the Church. It is possible to speak of the providential value of the translation of the LXX (and only of this ancient version), especially in its reception by the NT and early Christian theology, and to reserve the charism of inspiration for the authors.

The same terminology used by Saint John Chrysostom, quoted by Benoit, could be used without compromising the understanding of the charism of inspiration: The Holy Spirit has "inspired" Moses to compose the Scriptures, just as it has "inspired" Ezra to restore them, has "sent" the prophets and, finally, has "predisposed" the Seventy to translate.[36] In some way it is necessary to reserve an action of the Holy Spirit for those parts of the books of the LXX which differ or exceed in meaning or in text (Greek additions, whole books) relative to the Hebrew "originals" and which have been accepted by the NT or by early Christian theology as part of the road of revelation. What action of the Spirit are we talking about? As of now, it is problematic to speak of "inspiration" in this context.[37]

---

36. Cf. John Chrysostom, *Hom. Hebr.* 8.4.

37. Obviously it is not problematic to attribute the charism of inspiration to the Greek text of Wisdom and 2 Maccabees, which were composed directly in that language.

CHAPTER 7

A Word from the Church
The Decree of Trent

Now that the question which faced Jerome and Augustine has been posed, and I have put on the table the different factors at play, the hypotheses that bear on them, the reasons that go along with them and the aporias that they raise, the time has come to ask whether the Church, in its Magisterium, has said a firm word (with dogmatic value) that can guide us in this debate.

With regard to the textual problem, the Church has never said, nor has it had the temptation to say, "*this* is *the* Bible," pointing at a specific codex, or "*this* is *the* book of Isaiah," indicating a particular manuscript. It is another thing to be able to properly say: "this codex contains the Bible" or "this manuscript contains the book of Isaiah." From very early, Christian theologians have been aware of the textual plurality of the OT (both because of the matter of the polemic between the Hebrew and Greek texts and because of the presence of variants among the manuscripts of a single version) and of the need for a minimal practice of textual criticism.

It would be necessary to wait until the sixteenth century, and more specifically the Council of Trent, to witness, in a context of reaction to the Protestant Reformation, a dogmatic declaration of the canonical books that would involve reflection and a certain decisiveness with regard to the textual problem of both the OT and the NT. The decree which interests us was the first one of the fourth session, promulgated on April 8, 1546. We will take some time to study it as it touches on the question of the text of the OT.

Indeed, the principle of *Sola Scriptura* had made the Protestant Reformers feel the need to define the outlines of the Bible, such that, with regard to the OT, they limited it to the books of the Hebrew Bible, while rejecting, against most tradition, those we know as deuterocanonical. It was more than natural that one of the first tasks of the Council of Trent was to establish, with a dogmatic declaration, a list of canonical books which would include those rejected by the Protestants.

The preparation of the list did not start from zero, and not so much because of the weight of the many provincial councils or local synods, starting in the fourth century, which supported the "long" canon, for, in fact, the existence of other provincial councils which had opted for the "short" canon neutralized this argument.[1] The reason must be sought in a declaration of the Council of Florence, held a century earlier. In its decree "for the Jacobites" (1441), it had listed the books of the long canon of the OT. It was an ecumenical Council (and prior to the Protestant Reformation), for which reason in Trent no discussions or justifications were necessary regarding the list of canonical books.[2]

Now, the listing of the canonical books of the OT was not enough to close the debate which the Protestant Churches had opened with their choice of the canon of the Hebrew Bible. Both the Jews and the Protestants reject as non-canonical some parts of the protocanonical books which are common to all. It is not enough, therefore, to say that Daniel and Esther are canonical books to settle the problem. Are the parts of Esther which are only preserved in Greek canonical? Are the books of Susanna and Bel and the Dragon canonical, which appear in the Vulgate as chapters 13 and 14 of Daniel?

---

1. In the East, the Council of Laodicea of Phrygia (364) defended the restricted Hebrew canon, while in the West the Roman Council (382), under the authority of Pope Saint Damasus, and the letter of Pope Innocent I to Exuperius, bishop of Toulouse (405), presents the long list. The long canon would also be endorsed by the African Councils of Hippo (393) and I and II of Carthage (397 and 419). Two centuries later the ambiguity continued when the Council of Trullo (692) ratified equally the—different—canons of Laodicea and Carthage.

2. Cf. Michel, *Décrets du Concile de Trente*, 3–5, 16–17. Even so, during the debates prior to the decree of Trent about the canon, the question of the authority of the decree for the Jacobites of the Council of Florence arose since, in the opinion of one of the conciliar bishops, it had been promulgated after the dissolution of the synodal assembly. His opinion was refuted by another of those present (cf. Michel, *Décrets du Concile de Trente*, 3n2).

The conciliar fathers decided not specify the particular, canonical parts which are the object of discussion. To do so would have been very risky, since some parts might have been left out, especially from the NT, which they had perhaps not noticed.[3] The final decision, when discerning the canonical parts in question, was to refer to the reading tradition in the Catholic Church and to the presence of these parts in a particular edition which, in the opinion of the conciliar fathers, would be the authoritative expression of that tradition. Therefore, after listing the canonical books of the OT and the NT, the decree continues:

> Si quis autem libros ipsos integros cum omnibus suis partibus, prout in Ecclesia catholica legi consueverunt et in veteri vulgata latina editione habentur, pro sacris et canonicis non susceperit, et traditiones praedictas sciens et prudens contempserit: anatema sit.
>
> But if any one receive not, as sacred and canonical, the said books entire with all their parts, as they have been used to be read in the Catholic Church, and as they are contained in the old Latin vulgate edition; and knowingly and deliberately contemn the traditions aforesaid; let him be anathema.

The expression "integros cum omnibus suis partibus," when it refers, in the case of the OT, to the protocanonical books, is at the very heart of the textual question of interest here. Not only as it touches on the books of Esther and Daniel, already mentioned, but because of how it appears to resolve the textual problems which exist in other books. But in order for the expression "integros cum omnibus suis partibus" not to turn out to be ambiguous, and bearing in mind that the mention of the ecclesiastical reading tradition could turn out to be equally ambiguous and that the Council did not wish to list the "parts" in question, it was necessary to indicate an edition of books (a "Bible") which would serve as a pattern. The Council specified that edition: the Latin Vulgate which had been dominant in the West for several centuries.[4]

Was the Council not giving into the temptation, described above, to indicate a certain codex and to say "this is the Bible"? Not at all. As the

---

3. Cf. Michel, *Décrets du Concile de Trente*, 18.

4. The name *Vulgata* to identify a Latin edition which refers largely to Jerome's work of translation would take many years to become usual. In Jerome's time, and for some centuries more, the *editio Vulgata* identified the Latin version which today we know as the *Vetus*, which in the OT translates from the Greek of the LXX (Cf. Loewe, "Medieval History," 108).

second decree of this session of the Council would indicate,[5] and as the subsequent Magisterium would clarify,[6] the reference to the Vulgate in this first decree only had the intention of identifying an authoritative expression of the ecclesiastical reading tradition as far as the number of canonical books and their parts was concerned. This was far from the Council affirming that the Bible is in Latin and prohibiting reference to the Hebrew text or to the Greek of the LXX.[7]

5. "Moreover, the same sacred and holy Synod,—considering that no small utility may accrue to the Church of God, if it be made known which out of all the Latin editions, now in circulation, of the sacred books, is to be held as authentic,—ordains and declares, that the said old and vulgate edition, which, by the lengthened usage of so many years, has been approved of in the Church, be, in public lectures, disputations, sermons and expositions, held as authentic" (General Council of Trent, *Fourth Session*, 19). What is at stake is settling on one Latin edition among the many that are circulating, some of which are of low quality.

6. "The Professor, following the tradition of antiquity, will make use of the Vulgate as his text; for the Council of Trent decreed that 'in public lectures, disputations, preaching, and exposition,' the Vulgate is the 'authentic' version; and this is the existing custom of the Church. At the same time, the other versions which Christian antiquity has approved, should not be neglected, more especially the more ancient manuscripts" (*Providentissimus Deus*, EB 106); "The Council of Trent, in order to cope with the confusion occasioned by the new translations into Latin and into the vernacular languages which then spread, intended to sanction the public use, in the Western Church, of the Latin Vulgate version, justifying it by the age-old use which the Church has made of it. But by this it did not have in mind to reduce the authority of the ancient versions used in the Eastern Churches, especially of the LXX, used by the apostles themselves, and less still the authority of the original texts, and for this reason it resisted the will of some of the [conciliar] Fathers who wanted the exclusive use of the Vulgate as the only one authorized. . . . In summary, the Council of Trent declared the Vulgate 'authentic' in a juridical sense, that is, in what concerns the 'vis probativa in rebus fidei et morum,' but it did not exclude, in fact, possible divergences in relation to the original and to the ancient versions" (*Letter from the Pontifical Biblical Commission*, EB 526-27). "And if the Tridentine Synod wished 'that all should use as authentic' the Vulgate Latin version, this, as all know, applies only to the Latin Church and to the public use of the same Scriptures; nor does it, doubtless, in any way diminish the authority and value of the original texts" (*Divino afflante Spiritu*, EB 549).

7. In fact, in one of the meetings for discussion of the first decree it was considered very desirable to have available corrected editions of the Latin Vulgate, the Greek text (of the LXX) and the Hebrew (it should be recalled that there was already a printed Catholic edition of the Masoretic Hebrew text in the Complutensian Polyglot sponsored by Cardinal Cisneros, published in 1517) (cf. Michel, *Décrets du Concile de Trente*, 9). Furthermore, in the discussions about the second decree, about the authenticity of the Vulgate, it was even proposed that a Greek edition and a Hebrew one should also be declared authentic, but this idea was ultimately rejected because, at base, the decree was intended to bring order to the various Latin editions and indicate one to use in "public

However, it is legitimate to think that the decree of Trent, by indicating the Vulgate, and with the expression "integros cum omnibus suis partibus," "canonizes" certain of its textual choices. Bearing in mind that the book of Jeremiah has disputed "parts" (major sections do not appear in the Greek version of the LXX), the decree of Trent canonizes the long version, the one which appears in the Vulgate (which, in turn, translates the extended edition of the Proto-Masoretic text) which, after all, includes the short version attested by the LXX.[8]

The reference to the Vulgate in this conciliar decree, as an edition which resolves the textual questions linked to the canon, obliges us to take a look at this version as it was presented to the eyes of the conciliar fathers. At first glance, the mention of the Latin version, linked to Jerome's work of translation, could give us to understand that, with the passage of time, in the Church the *hebraica veritas* supported by the monk of Bethlehem became dominant. However, the edition of the Vulgate which was on the table in the conciliar sessions was not by any means "the Bible" which Jerome had desired, to the point that in its arrangement the *Septuaginta auctoritas* played an important role, as will be seen below. In a certain way it can be said that the Vulgate, by blending the two principles which were at odds, is presented as a work of synthesis.

---

lectures, disputations, preaching, and exposition." That is, it had to do with questions in the Latin-language churches (cf. Muñoz Iglesias, "Decreto tridentino," 140–41).

8. It is fair to recognize that there is an open discussion about whether or not it was the intention of the Council of Trent to give an authoritative word about the canonicity of the smallest parts in dispute: "Sur ces principes qui sont expressément promulgués par le concile, se greffent des questions proprement théologiques, dans lesquelles des opinions divergentes ont encore le droit de se produire. Il n'est pas démontré, en effet, que le concile de Trente ait voulu définir la canonicité des moindres détails renfermés dans le texte usuel" (Michel, *Décrets du Concile de Trente*, 23n1).

CHAPTER 8

The Latin Vulgate
A Work of Synthesis

IN ORDER TO UNDERSTAND the process that led to the formation of a specific Latin edition of biblical books which the Council of Trent knew as the *Vulgate* it is necessary to start with Jerome's work of translation, restricted to the text of the OT, as has been done so far.

JEROME'S WORK OF TRANSLATION: THE STARTING POINT

It must be remembered that the doctor of Bethlehem had made as many as two Latin versions of particular books: a revision of the *Vetus Latina* on the basis of the fifth column of Origen and a translation *ex novo* from the Hebrew. This latter translation was completed for all the books which were circulating in Hebrew or Aramaic in the year 406. It is known that Jerome had available a team of scribes who copied his works as they were finished and sent them to wherever they were in demand. When those works reached their destination new copies were made and in this way the new translations of the Dalmatian began to circulate throughout Latin Christendom.

It is important to realize that what was coming out of Bethlehem was nothing more than individual copies which contained the translation of a single book. It is an anachronism to think that Jerome concluded the composition of a codex which contained his complete Latin Bible and that it later began to be copied. Nor does the idea that the holy doctor was carrying out an assignment from Pope Saint Damasus by translating anew the whole Bible (and still less from the Hebrew) correspond to reality, such that his books were being awaited by everyone to make up the new Latin Bible. An assignment like this was given only for the gospels, in the period when Jerome was in Rome.

At the death of Saint Jerome (although in fact already earlier, as Augustine attests in their correspondence) a battle began which was basically played out by geographical areas, between the old Latin translation and the new ones that were coming from Jerome. Bearing in mind that in any case they were translations (and therefore revisable) and considering that Christianity has never felt a special imperative to preserve the biblical text without error,[1] it is not surprising that the textual traditions of the different Latin versions of a single book should have gotten mixed together, because of the simple fact that in many cases the copyists (or commentators) introduced into one manuscript readings from another which seemed more suitable to them. It is true that this mixture affected the NT more (given that the two versions were similar because they were based on the same Greek text), but a transfer of readings can also be identified in the books of the OT.

With regard to the number of books which a Latin edition of the OT should contain, another piece of information to be borne in mind is that pandects, that is, the editions which contained all the books of the Bible in one codex, were very scarce in the centuries that followed the death of Jerome. The manuscripts which circulated contained a single book of the Bible or sometimes collections of "homogenous" books, like the four gospels, for the NT, or the Octateuch, for the OT. Thus it became evident that the edition which would be known as the *Vulgate* and of which Trent now says that it "by the lengthened usage of so many years, has been approved of in the Church,"[2] would sooner or later have to make a choice not only of the text type, but also of the number of books. And all of this without

---

1. The textual transmission of the Bible (OT and NT) in Christian circles has produced innumerable variants both in the manuscripts in the original languages and in the versions, unlike the transmission of the Hebrew Bible in the Jewish context, where the care of the copyists not to introduce errors reached unsuspected limits. The idea that the text contained a revelation not only in its content but in its form supported that drive to not change anything, the expression of which is the Masoretic apparatus, especially the *masora finalis* which closes each book (in which a count of the words and even the consonants is done). Cf. Martín Contreras and Seijas de los Ríos, *Masora*.

2. "Haec ipsa vetus et vulgata editio, quae longo tot saeculorum uso in ipsa ecclesia probata est" (General Council of Trent, *Fourth Session*, EB 61).

the mediation of a magisterial decision: the text and the number of books gained dominance, little by little, in Western Christendom. I will identify the basic stages in this process.

HOW WAS THE VULGATE "MADE"? HOW DID IT BECOME DOMINANT?

In order to facilitate the clarity of this review, nothing would be better than to start at the stage which, in the end, turned out to be key, so as to look both backward and forward from it.[3] This is the reign of Charlemagne, who began in 768 as king of the Franks and ended in 814 as head of the Holy Roman Germanic Empire (crowned as emperor by Pope Leo III on Christmas Day in 800). The desire to restore what had been the Roman Empire in fact facilitated a certain unity in a large part of European territory, not only politically but also through a resurgence of Latin culture and art, promoted by the Carolingian emperor himself. The vigorous presence of Islam on the Iberian Peninsula and in North Africa left these areas out of the new order, and they were precisely those areas in which the *Vetus Latina* had resisted the pressure of the new Vulgate.

Among the commands of Charlemagne directed toward promoting religion and culture, one in particular is of interest here, directed toward bringing order to the state of corruption in which many manuscripts for liturgical use were found. Aware that the copies of biblical manuscripts were being made by people without experience, Charlemagne decreed in 789 that all copies of the Gospels and the Psalms (the books most used in the liturgy) were to be made with care by expert scribes (*perfectae aetatis homines scribant cum omni diligentia*).[4]

Unlike what happened in the case of Pope Damasus' assignment to Jerome, in the present case no commission is found from Charlemagne to a particular ecclesiastic to make a corrected and unified edition of the Vulgate. To fulfill the royal command, different initiatives emerged which sought to clean the manuscripts of errors, conflations, interpolations and

---

3. In this review I follow the informed and lengthy article of Loewe, "Medieval History," as well as the reference works in this field: Berger, *Histoire de la Vulgate*; Fischer, *Lateinische Bibelhandschriften*.

4. The decrees of Charlemagne which interest us, together with the history of the reforms in the biblical field which were carried out in his time, are found in Fischer, *Lateinische Bibelhandschriften*, 101–202 (101).

secondary readings which had accumulated in them over the course of time. One of these initiatives, the one which ended up becoming dominant due to the prestige of its mentor and the quality of his *scriptorium*, was that of Alcuin of York.[5] Born near York (then part of the kingdom of Northumbria, in the British Isles), in 782 Alcuin was appointed head of the Palatine School of Charlemagne in Aachen and, subsequently, in 796, abbot of Saint Martin of Tours, where he began his recension of the Vulgate and where he would die in 804.

Limiting myself now to Alcuin's initiative, it is plain that a job of manuscript correction can only be done if one has a textual "point of arrival" toward which to be inclined; in textual criticism this implies the presence of ancient, trustworthy manuscripts with which to make comparisons. It is here that the textual choices begin, the first of which is the choice between the tradition of the *Vetus* (translated from the Greek of the LXX) and the Vulgate (translated from the Hebrew).

The presence in the recension of Alcuin of the textual tradition which proceeds from Jerome's work of translation from the Hebrew should not by any means be attributed to the personal taste of the abbot of Saint Martin of Tours. He did no more than put forward the tradition which he had received, with its additions cleaned up. Indeed, Jerome's version had made its way into a large part of Western Christendom, especially by means of its predominant presence in Italy and in a good part of the liturgical tradition that was spreading through Europe. As I said above, the areas where the *Vetus* was most resistant to giving way, like *Hispania* and North Africa, little by little became isolated from the future empire.

The textual tradition which Alcuin puts forward is linked to his birthplace, in the county of Yorkshire, where the Latin manuscripts of the Bible belong to the Northumbrian text type, linked in turn to one of the recensions of Cassiodorus (485–580), a native of Squillace (a city in Calabria, Italy). That recension, in codex form, was taken to Northumbria, from where it exercised its textual influence over that region and over a good

---

5. For a complete study of this Bible and its history, cf. Fischer, *Lateinische Bibelhandschriften*, 203–403. Other important initiatives contemporary with Alcuin were the recension made by Theodulf (760–821), bishop of Orleans, and that of Maurdramnus, abbot of Corbie between about 772 and 780. In addition, there remain textual traces of other corrections situated at the end of the eighth century. Charlemagne was referring to all these initiatives when he stated in 801 that already some time earlier the text of the OT and NT had been corrected (*iam pridem universos veteris ac novi instrumenti libros, librariourum imperitia depravatos, Deo nos in omnibus adiuvante, examussim correximus*) (cf. Loewe, "Medieval History," 134).

part of Europe through the Anglo-Saxon missionaries. As regards the protocanonical books, this recension contained the translation which Jerome made from the Hebrew.

However, the Alcuin's Bible contains one exception: the Psalter which it includes is not the *Psalterium iuxta hebraicam veritatem* but the *Psalterium iuxta LXX*. In fact, the exception is due to the low popularity enjoyed by the version of Psalms which Jerome made from the Hebrew, which was practically unused in the liturgy.[6] What version was used? Depending on the geographical zones, recitations were done from the Psalter of the *Vetus Latina*, from the Roman Psalter (a correction of the Psalms of the *Vetus* done by Jerome in his Roman period, in the years 382–385) or from the Psalter *iuxta LXX* (or Gallican Psalter, also a work by Jerome who translated from the Greek fifth column of the Hexapla). In all three cases we are looking at Latin translations which come from the Greek version of the LXX. In all likelihood, the fact that the NT often quotes according to the form of the LXX, together with the force of custom linked to a book recited daily in the liturgy, kept Jerome's new version from the Hebrew from ever managing to displace the earlier ones.

The Roman Psalter was the text used in Rome, as well as in the center and south of Italy. From there it entered with the missionaries into England, and later from the islands it spread, with the new missionaries, to a good part of the continent. For its part, the Psalter of the *Vetus*, in different recensions, prevailed in the north of Italy (*Psalterium Ambrosianum*), Hispania (*Psalterium Mozarabicum*) and Gaul. Curiously, the Gallican Psalter only found a welcome in Ireland, where it began to prevail in the liturgy starting in 600, and contemporaneously in a part of Gaul under the influence of Gregory of Tours. Both centers were decisive in helping this Psalter to wind up becoming dominant through Alcuin's Bible.

Indeed, the impressive presence of Irish monks on the continent in the 7th century, who were in demand in monasteries and schools because of their classical training (which included mastery of Greek), caused their biblical manuscripts, and particularly their liturgical Psalter, to spread,

---

6. "Das *Iuxta Hebraeos* wurde in der Liturgie nie praktisch gebraucht, war aber bis Alkuin Bestandteil der Ganzbibeln und diente als Hilfsmittel für die Wissenschaft, besonders in den doppelten, dreifachen, ja vierfachen Psalterien, in denen die verschiedenen Psalmtexte nebeinandergestellt wurden" (Fischer, *Lateinische Bibelhandschriften*, 343). Even so, the Bible of Theodulf contained the edition of the Psalter *iuxta Hebraeos*, perhaps because of the more erudite nature of his work (cf. Fischer, *Lateinische Bibelhandschriften*, 342).

especially in Western and Nordic Europe, and it gave them more weight in comparison to other textual traditions.[7] Moreover, the presence of the Gallican Psalter in France (both because of the influence of Gregory of Tours and because of that of the Irish monks) was decisive in causing the Carolingian reform, and more specifically Alcuin (who, it must not be forgotten, was the abbot of Saint Martin of Tours), to finally decide in favor of it.

Alcuin's work was completed in the summer of 800 and was presented to the emperor in Rome on the occasion of his coronation, on the 25th of December of the same year. One of the advantages of the *scriptorium* of Saint Martin of Tours, which surely facilitated the success of its recension, was that it produced pandect editions or collections of all the books of the Bible in a single codex. Obviously, a collection of this type entails, as it does for the text type, a choice: Which books should be put in? Which should be left out?

In this decision, Alcuin does no more than again refer to tradition, and in this case the *Septuaginta auctoritas* gets its revenge: the books of the Bible whose Hebrew original was lost (or those which originated directly in Greek) continued to be read (and quoted) in the West after Jerome. Alcuin's collection of books takes in the long canon attested by the Greek editions of the LXX.

If we now turn our gaze ahead, we will see how the prestige of the *scriptorium* of Tours, at the head of the *scriptoria carolingios*, and the beauty and quality of its ornamented Bibles, made it easier for the text that they contained to become dominant and to be copied for use in different regions of the empire. In this way, Alcuin's text came to have a kind of authority which was tacitly recognized by the printers of the first Latin Bible (1456), who combined the text type coming out of Tours with the order of books and the division into chapters of the important Parisian text or Paris Bible (early 13th century), which in turn unites the text of Alcuin with the influence of the Irish monastic tradition, which was not far from the Northumbrian text type. This first printed edition, for obvious reasons, was widely

---

7. "Irish houses had succeeded in maintaining some classical learning: a knowledge of Greek was, in northern and western Europe, effectively an Irish monopoly, and the Irish bible carries signs of correction made immediately from the Greek text. Irish learning was prized, and the Irish sufficiently sought after as teachers for aspiring pupils even to go to Ireland themselves to seek them out. Indeed, in the seventh century no continental monastery of any importance was without some Irish link" (Loewe, "Medieval History," 130).

disseminated, and it was the one that came down to the presidency of the Council of Trent.

THE VULGATE, A WORK OF SYNTHESIS

After this review we are prepared to understand in what sense the Vulgate, as it was received in Trent and used in Western Christendom for more than a thousand years, unites the two principles at odds, the *hebraica veritas* and the *Septuaginta auctoritas*, forming a true work of *synthesis*. The books whose Hebrew (or Aramaic) original Jerome knew, enter the Vulgate in the translation done by the monk of Bethlehem from that language. The rest of the books of the long canon, which were peculiar to the Septuagint, are not left out, but enter in the old Latin translation of the *Vetus* or the revision of this which Jerome did.

In order to reinforce the synthetic nature of the Vulgate edition which would come to be dominant in the Latin West, the collection of books includes, as I have indicated, a very significant exception to the principle state above: the Psalter. Indeed, the translation of Psalms which enters the new Latin edition is the one that comes from the LXX and not from the Hebrew "original." The exception is significant because the reason for this anomaly is found in another of the principles which, curiously, both Jerome and Augustine claimed for themselves: the use of the OT in the NT.

We have already had occasion to see how a good part of the theology of the NT is constructed on the basis of passages of the OT, many of them according to the Greek version of the LXX, when it differs from the Hebrew Proto-Masoretic text. Well, a significant number of these latter passages are found in the Psalms.[8] I previously presented the example of Psalm 40 (LXX 39:7), which is decisive for the theology of divine sonship in the letter to the Hebrews. Of equal importance are passages from Psalms 8 (8:6), 16 (LXX 15:10) and 110 (LXX 109:1, 3), in all cases according to the version of the LXX.[9]

It is more than understandable that the monks, familiar with the theology of the NT, should have wanted to recite the Psalter daily according to

---

8. Cf. Attridge and Fassler, *Psalms in Community*; Dodd, *According to the Scriptures*; Grelot, *Mystère du Christ*; Moyise and Menken, *Psalms in the New Testament*.

9. Urassa, *Psalm 8*; Klein, "Zur Wirkungsgeschichte von Psalm 8"; Childs, "Psalm 8"; Kilgallen, "Use of Psalm"; Juel, "Social Dimensions"; Boers, "Psalm 16"; Hay, *Glory at the Right Hand*; Loader, "Christ at the Right Hand."

a version which would not contradict those key passages of the final testament. In this way, the use in the liturgy of the versions coming from the LXX (*Vetus*, Roman Psalter and Gallican Psalter) first became dominant. Later on, one of them, the Gallican Psalter, would impose it dominance over the rest in all the editions of the Vulgate.

CHAPTER 9

Lessons from the Past for Overcoming the Polemic

A PULL REDIRECTED TO UNITY

The mention of the Vulgate in the decree of Trent about the canon has made us look back over this Latin edition which, in its form, shows a synthesis of the two principles which can be called "Catholic": the pull toward the "original text" (contained in the expression *hebraica veritas*) and the pull toward the choices of the apostolic tradition, which are especially brought together in the NT (contained in the expression *Septuaginta auctoritas*).

Neither principle can be easily rejected. A translation cannot replace, *tout court*, the text in its original language, for reasons that are not only linguistic (every version must refer to an original before which it is continuously validated) but theological (the charism of the inspiration cannot avoid reference to the original text which is the product of that same gift). Moreover, the fullness of revelation is achieved in Christ, of whom the NT is the written and inspired testimony. It is necessary to pay attention to the reception of the OT given by the apostolic tradition (present in the NT), which includes a certain development of the Scriptures that runs through expressions, passages, sections and books of the Greek version of the LXX.

It should not be hidden that there exists a tension between the two principles, as I have in fact been able to prove in the description of its unfolding in history. But the particularity of that which is Catholic is found precisely in having united two poles which are in tension, as is shown in the two apparently irreconcilable statements of a dogma: Triune, in the divine

Mystery; God and man, in Christology; virgin and mother, in Mariology. The contrary, the unilateral affirmation of one of the poles, while denying the other, characterizes heresy.

Bridging the gap, the Vulgate, in what is paradigmatic about it according to Trent (certainly not in its Latin language), unites the principles we have seen "at war" at the hands of Jerome and Augustine. In that sense it is possible to speak of a work of Catholic synthesis.

In the presentation of the polemic between the two great doctors, I excluded what the late position of Augustine was, once the echoes of his diatribe with Jerome had died away. Now is the time to bring it in, since it is inspired by the same principle of synthesis to which I am referring.

The aforementioned late position finds expression in his work *De civitate Dei*, specifically in its book XVIII, dated around the year 425, five years after the death of Jerome.[1] It is true that in book XVIII, as we have already seen above, Augustine energetically argues for the authority of the LXX and its inspired nature, but he does it while being already aware of the value of the Hebrew text for which Jerome was arguing and not in contrast to it. When commenting on the particular edition of the LXX in the fifth column of the Hexapla of Origen (a version which Jerome himself had partially translated into Latin), which included with asterisks those passages which only appeared in the Hebrew text, Augustine states:

> Consequently if, as is proper, we do not see in those Scriptures anything but what the Spirit of God has said through men, it is apparent that whatever is found in the Hebrew text and not in the Seventy, the Spirit of God did not intend to say through the latter, but through the former prophets. On the other hand, whatever is found in the Seventy, and is lacking in Hebrew, the same Spirit intended to say through the former rather than the latter, thus manifesting that both these and those were prophets. In the same manner he said, as it pleased him, some things through Isaiah, others through Jeremiah, others through one prophet, others through another, and also the same things in a different manner through this one or the other one. Thus, as much as is found in these and in those, one and the same Spirit intended to say it through these

---

1. The work *De civitate Dei*, consisting of twenty-two books, began to be composed in 412 and was concluded in 426. Some pieces of information which Augustine himself provides in other writings make it possible to proceed to fix the chronology of the composition of the different books. Thus it is possible to situate the composition of book XVIII in the year 425. Cf. Trapè, "Introduzione Generale," xvi–xvii; Trapè, *Agostino*, 267.

and those; but in such a manner that the former went before in prophecy and the latter afterward interpreted prophetically.[2]

In some way the mature or late position of Augustine can be described as synthetic, in the sense that it accepts and unites in one single will of the Spirit that which is exclusive to the Hebrew text and that which is only attested by the LXX. In the following chapter he returns to this synthetic principle, in this case on the basis of the fact that the NT (and therefore "the apostles") quotes the OT both from the Hebrew and from the Greek of the LXX:

> Therefore I too, following with my dim understanding the tracks of the apostles, since they also took the testimonies of the prophets from Hebrew and from the Seventy, judged it suitable to make use of both this authority and that one, since both are the same and divine one.[3]

The Hebrew text and the Greek text of the LXX come to share in the same divine authority. The dialectical tension which dominated the early correspondence between Jerome and Augustine rests on the synthetic unity which the one from Hippo achieves in his final years of life.[4] It is fair to recognize that Augustine would never have achieved this position without the work of Origen (the Hexapla) and without the work of translation of Jerome, which put before the bishop of Hippo a text, the Hebrew, to whose authority he had not until then paid attention.

THE MODEL OF THE POLYGLOT BIBLE

In our day, Barthélemy, by explicitly taking up again the position of Augustine, launches a proposal which can also be described as synthetic:

> To close this exposition, nothing remains to me but to propose, with Saint Augustine, a Bible with two columns as an original form of the Christian Old Testament: one would contain the Septuagint of the early centuries of our era, the other the Hebrew text which the scribes of Israel canonized.[5]

---

2. Augustine, *Civ.* 18.43.

3. Augustine, *Civ.* 18.44.

4. "Nella maturità del *De Civitate* il fervore dogmatico della lettera 494/95 cede il posto alla duplicità esegetica" (Veltri, "L'ispirazione della LXX," 59).

5. Barthélemy, "Place de la Septante," 28.

Hebraica veritas versus Septuaginta auctoritatem

The Bible (OT) with two columns which Barthélemy proposes is, obviously, a polyglot Bible. His proposal intends to overcome an exclusive contrast or a mere sterile juxtaposition. The polyglot Bible format is not new. What represents a novelty is the insistence on again taking up the textual plurality of the Bible in an age dominated by literary criticism which for two centuries has tended to confuse what is primitive with what is pure and original, and the later developments with what is decadent or sclerotic.[6]

If we study some history, the first Bible that can rightly be called a polyglot is the *diglot* (Hebrew-Greek) of Origen, that is, his Hexapla, which displays in six columns four Greek versions plus the Proto-Masoretic Hebrew text and its Greek transliteration. I have already commented above on the decisive role that this edition had for the origin and development of the polemic between Jerome and Augustine, as well as for arriving at the final synthetic position of the latter.

It would be necessary to wait more than twelve centuries to again see a publishing project of this nature, which was the one that really began the series of polyglot Bibles. I am referring to the Complutensian Polyglot Bible (1514–17), sponsored by Cardinal Cisneros, published in Alcalá, this time on a printing press, in six volumes.[7] The first volume displays the Pentateuch in four languages: Hebrew, Greek, Latin and Aramaic. On each page, the outer column presents the Masoretic (vocalized) Hebrew text, the center column the Latin text of the Vulgate, the inner column the Greek text of the Septuagint (with interlinear Latin translation) and in the lower part of all three columns appears the Aramaic text of Targum Onkelos, accompanied by a Latin version.

Cisneros' project belongs to an era of returning to the sources which, while not displacing the Latin Vulgate (it was an initiative of the Catholic Latin West) recovered, surprisingly, the Hebrew text which only the Jews were transmitting, the Greek Septuagint which was read in the Christian

---

6. This trend has been clear, since the end of the nineteenth century, in the study of the sources of the Pentateuch and in the study of the formation of the prophetic books (cf. Carbajosa, *Faith*, especially the chapters "Research on the Formation of the Pentateuch" and "The Critical Study of the Prophets"). With regard to the NT, the same trend can be discerned in the identification of what was original in Jesus with the Q source in the gospels (cf. Brown, *Introduction*, 116–23; Foster, "'Q' Myth"). In some way this same mindset is the one that tends to consider the version of the LXX as a late stage, loaded with interpretations, far from the original purity of the Hebrew.

7. For a complete and recent study of this edition, cf. Carbajosa and García Serrano, *Una Biblia a varias voces*.

East, and the Aramaic Targumim, which had never been used in the Church.[8]

The Bible of Alcalá was to inaugurate an era which saw a succession of publishing projects that went on enriching the concept of the Polyglot Bible with new texts and versions. The Antwerp Polyglot or *Biblia Regia* (1569-72), under the direction of Benito Arias Montano, in eight volumes, incorporated, as a new feature, the Syriac Peshitta, and it completed the Aramaic Targumim which in the Complutensian Polyglot only covered the Pentateuch. Then in the seventeenth century there were published the Polyglot Bibles of Paris (1629-45), in ten volumes, and London (1653-57), in six. The first incorporated the Samaritan Pentateuch and an Arabic version of the OT. The second, which was the most complete and which would enjoy the most success, was published by Brian Walton and incorporated the Ethiopic version.

The eighteenth and nineteenth centuries would see the growth of philological scholarship, and they would witness a multiplication of partial editions on the basis of the appearance of new manuscripts, both of the OT and of the NT. With regard to the OT, this whole movement cause the ideal of the Polyglot Bible to be forgotten[9] and, by the twentieth century, for scholarship to be directed toward the independent production of critical editions of each text or version. In some way, all the partial investigations were directed toward a common objective: to arrive at the stage which was the most ancient, or closest to the "original" of each book of the Hebrew Bible.[10] In this sense, the ancient versions tended to be seen as witnesses to different stages of development of the Hebrew text and as a source of information for the textual criticism of the Hebrew Bible. The wealth of the different columns of a Polyglot came to be enclosed in the critical apparatus of a Hebrew text.[11]

---

8. To understand the reach of Cisneros' work, cf. Carbajosa, "A los 500 años."

9. Cf. Hendel, "From Polyglot to Hypertext," 28-29.

10. The discovery of the biblical manuscripts of Qumran, starting in 1947, relaunched the ideal of the search for the original text by putting on the table, with regard to the Hebrew Bible, testimonies which preceded by a thousand years those which until then were available (the oldest were from the ninth-eleventh centuries C.E.).

11. Paradigmatic in this sense is the edition of the Hebrew Bible dominant in the academic field, which has been the basis for most modern translations of the OT: the *Biblia Hebraica*, edited by Kittel (BHK, 1929-37), replaced by the *Biblia Hebraica Stuttgartensia* (BHS, 1966-77), which, in turn, is being prepared in a new edition, in progress, the *Biblia Hebraica Quinta* (BHQ, 2004-). In these editions the MT as it appears in the *Codex Leningradensis* is presented and a rich critical apparatus is provided, with variants

Although Barthélemy's proposal goes back to 1967, only recently, in the last few decades, has the way again become open to the idea of a Polyglot Bible, or in contemporary technical terms, the idea of a single Bible attested in Hebrew manuscripts and ancient versions. Both text-critical studies and theological and hermeneutical reflection have contributed to this openness.

In the first case it may seem paradoxical that a discipline which had promoted the search for the most original Hebrew stage of the Bible should have wound up pointing to a polyglot synopsis as the most suitable form of understanding the relationship between different editions of the Bible.[12] Actually, the advance in text-critical studies has revealed that it is impossible, as well as naive, to reconstruct the "original" of a biblical text. Not only because we do not have enough manuscript information but also because in many cases we are faced with different editions (more or less clear, more or less extensive) of a single book which require an external agency to determine which text is considered sacred or canonical for a community.

This last is a consideration which actually enters into the field of hermeneutics, another of the disciplines which has opened the way for the idea of a polyglot Bible. Indeed, beyond the information that certain differences between witnesses to a single book are due to different editions and not to the logic of original and secondary readings (as in the previously studied case of Jeremiah), the development of the biblical text (OT), and even its transmission and translation, has gone through stages which pertain to the growth of the testimony of Revelation, obviously before the period of the NT. Again, only an agency with authority, external to the text, can determine which developments are canonical. It is not a matter of a "subjective" or random agency: the very historical event of Jesus Christ, attested in the NT, establishes the point of arrival of the preceding revelation and becomes the ultimate criterion for the reception of the prior processes which point to it.

---

from the Masoretic tradition itself, from the Qumran manuscripts and from the ancient versions.

12. The height of this paradox is found in the edition of the book of Jeremiah in the project *The Hebrew Bible: A Critical Edition* (which at first bore the name *Oxford Hebrew Bible*) which intends to arrive at an eclectic text which is as close as possible to the Hebrew original. In the case of Jeremiah this project must recognize that it is looking at two different editions, for which reason it presents two Hebrew texts (one of them is supposed to be the Hebrew Vorlage of LXX Jeremiah) in a double column (cf. Crawford et al., "Sample Editions").

Lessons from the Past for Overcoming the Polemic

Today there are numerous authors who are calling for a "Bible in several voices"[13] and numerous projects which seek to make this reality. With regard to the former it will suffice to quote two who have enormous prestige in the field of biblical textual criticism. I am referring to Adrian Schenker and Emanuel Tov. It is curious that these two authors, who are directly involved in "critical" editions of the Bible Hebrew,[14] and who at this time could be considered the two greatest authorities on biblical textual criticism, through two different paths are calling for a change of direction in studies which will accommodate the textual plurality of the Bible.

Schenker, who is Catholic (a Dominican religious), based on his knowledge of textual diversity, and out of a canonical and theological concern, founded on the study of the patristic tradition, states:

> Since the Scriptures present a certain irreducible textual diversity, it is necessary to understand the textual form of the Scriptures not as a song with a single voice, but as a polyphonic song.[15]

A polyphonic song, in the first instance, refers to the Proto-Masoretic Hebrew text and the Greek version of the LXX, since Schenker frames this statement in the context of the dialogues of Origen with Julius Africanus and of Jerome with Augustine. However, in the same article, Schenker opens the "score" to other ancient versions, like the Syriac Peshitta, the Latin Vulgate, and the Ethiopic, Coptic and Armenian versions, all of them linked to deeply rooted Christian communities, with their own languages, which have not had access to the Scriptures by any means other than their own version. This privilege would not be extended to the translations of the Bible in the modern era, which now has access to the biblical texts in Hebrew and Greek and to people trained to read them and translate them into their languages.[16]

Tov, who is Jewish, comes to the same conclusion by a different path. In spite of the fact that his cultural and hermeneutical tradition links him to the MT, Tov is well aware that that textual tradition is not *the* Bible. It is curious that it is he who reminds all the exegetes, including the Christian ones, of this:

---

13. Cf. "Prólogo" in Carbajosa and García Serrano, *Una Biblia a varias voces*, 11–12.

14. Schenker directs the committee which is editing the *Biblia Hebraica Quinta* and Tov has been part of the *Hebrew University Bible Project*.

15. Schenker, "L'Ècriture sainte," 180.

16. Cf. Schenker, "L'Ècriture sainte," 184–85.

> Although critical scholars, as opposed to the public at large, know that MT does not constitute *the* Bible, they nevertheless often approach it in this way. They base many critical commentaries and introductions mainly on MT; occasional remarks on other textual witnesses merely pay lip service to the notion that other texts exist.[17]

In Tov's opinion, this marked tendency is due to the preponderant role that the MT has had in the critical editions of the Bible, in which the important readings of the LXX, the Peshitta and the Qumran manuscripts were lost in complicated critical apparatuses. Although he is aware of the difficulties that it entails, Tov proposes an edition with several columns:

> The purpose of a multi-column edition would be to educate the users toward an egalitarian approach to the textual witnesses which cannot be achieved with the present tools. Such an edition would present MT, LXX, the SP, and some Qumran texts, on an equal basis in parallel columns. . . . The presentation of the text in the parallel columns would graphically show the relation between the plus and minus elements. Only by this means can future generations of scholars be expected to approach the textual data in an unbiased way, without MT forming the basis of their thinking.[18]

With regard to the projects which seek to make this ideal of a Bible with several columns a reality, we can distinguish between initiatives which encompass all the books of the Bible and partial initiatives, relating to a single book. Among the former I will highlight two: the project of the *École biblique et arquéologique française de Jérusalem* and some digital editions of the Bible. With respect to the latter, it is enough to say that the possibility of displaying the Hebrew texts and the different ancient versions in several columns makes these instruments (at least some of them) true Polyglot Bibles, with the advantage that the hyperlinks provide complementary information which can be displayed without losing sight of the whole.[19] I will take some time to describe the project of the *École biblique*.

Under the name of *La Bible en ses Traditions* (The Bible in its Traditions) is hidden an ambitious project which seeks to unite the critical study of the Bible (of which the *Jerusalem Bible* is one product) with the different traditions that have received, read, translated and interpreted it. As regards

---

17. Tov, "Hebrew Scripture Editions," 308.
18. Tov, "Hebrew Scripture Editions," 309–10.
19. Cf. Tov, "Electronic Scripture Editions."

the textual aspect, which is what interests us here, this project turns to the image of the "digital scroll" which is displayed from right to left and vice versa:

> What has inspired our choice [the digital scroll] is that it is a good means to be able to show the different versions of the sacred texts in parallel, verse by verse, as on a score of polyphonic music. In this way, the reader reads the Word of God in several voices, as we have received it down through the centuries. When the scroll is displayed, the letters "M," "G," "V" or "S" appear in the text, which refer to the origins of the translations of the sacred text, in its different Traditions: M from Masoretic (Hebrew), G for the Greek, V for the Vulgate (Latin) or S for the Syriac.[20]

This is a project which began in 2010 and which will still take years to complete.

The partial initiatives, which concern a single book are, obviously, simpler to do. Normally they have to do with books which have a special textual complexity, like Jeremiah,[21] Joshua[22] or 1–2 Kings. With regard to these last two books, Pablo Torijano Morales and Andrés Piquer Otero, professors at the Complutensian University, are preparing a polyglot-synoptic electronic edition which presents the following texts in columns: MT, Targum, Peshitta, Vulgate and the Hebrew text of Chronicles when it is parallel to Kings; LXX^A (hexaplaric text), LXX^B (majority text), LXX^L (Lucianic text), *Vetus Latina* and the Armenian, Georgian, Coptic and Ethiopic

---

20. The description of the project can be consulted online on the page of the *École biblique*: https://www.ebaf.edu/project-best/le-projet/ as well as on the page of *La Bible en ses Traditions*: https://scroll.bibletraditions.org.

21. Richard D. Weis, on the basis of the two textual forms of the book (the ones which MT and LXX preserve) states that "an ideal critical edition of these texts might take this form: a thoroughly tagged, annotated, commented and hyperlinked virtual polyglot that allows the user to manipulate the actual texts that come to us from Antiquity and information about them in order to approximate in actual, readable form the texts, once actual in Antiquity and pointed to by the actual evidence that has survived, but now only virtually accessible through the work of textual criticism" (Weis, "Jeremiah amid Actual and Virtual Editions," 385).

22. Kristin de Troyer ends an article about the textual plurality of the book of Joshua in this way: "The study of the textual plurality of the Book of Joshua would benefit from a modern digital Polyglot, in which at least the following texts need to be provided in a critical way: the OG, the MT, 4QJosh^a, and the Vetus Latina. It is thus time for a new project: the *Digital Complutensian Polyglot Bible*!" (Troyer, "Textual Plurality," 342).

versions, in addition to giving space to the material coming from Josephus and to the quotations from the Greek and Latin Fathers.²³

OVERCOMING A POLEMIC THAT COMES DOWN TO OUR DAY: PROMETHEUS VS. NARCISSUS

The review which has been done, culminating in the need for a plural approach to the biblical traditions, helps up to understand that an OT with several columns should not be judged as something negative or as a result of our imperfect knowledge of textual history.

The old polemic between Jerome and Augustine continues to be present in our day, bringing into confrontation, in this case, those who are looking for an *Urtext* which has as its starting point the Pre-Masoretic text, on the one hand, and those who argue for the Greek version of the LXX as *the* Christian Bible, the Bible of Tradition, on the other hand. Both groups feel uncomfortable with a solution (a Bible with several columns) which does not take the Bible back to a certain text or textual tradition (although in the respective cases it would be of a very different nature).

Very acutely, Giuseppe Veltri identifies in this polemic the tension between Prometheus and Narcissus.²⁴ As Prometheus stole fire from the gods, so a certain turn in modern textual criticism, and in the exegetical world in general, *intends* to arrive at the original form, in Hebrew, of the biblical revelation through the ever richer set of textual material and critical instruments, which were not available in the past.²⁵ In this operation of "climbing to the heights of heaven," the testimony of the ancient versions would be nothing more than a *subsidium* to arrive at a single text, the *Urtext*. This spirit is the one that lies beneath the "pan-Hebraism" which has dominated the biblical academic world from the second half of the nineteenth century

---

23. Cf. Tov, "Electronic Scripture Editions," 93. Cf. the need for and the spirit of this project in Piquer Otero and Torijano Morales, "מלכים, Βασιλειῶν, Reges," 351.

24. "La storia della valutazione teologico-autoritativa del testo AT in genere e della LXX in specie, vacilla ermeneuticamente tra Prometeo e Narciso: una ricerca puntigliosa e mediatrice volta a trarre dalla scrittura quell'universo vitale che la parola cela gelosamente nella sua formulazione, e un'autoriflessione tradizionale e dogmatica in una fluidità testuale ed ermeneutica" (Veltri, "L'ispirazione della LXX," 67).

25. "Many modern Christians are fixated with the search for an 'original text,' but from the beginning it was not so. . . . This is a distinctively modern theological anxiety" (Law, *When God Spoke Greek*, 168).

until almost the end of the twentieth century, and which tacitly identifies the OT with the Hebrew text, dealt with critically.[26]

For his part, Narcissus, in Greek mythology, fell in love with his own image, reflected in a pond, and he became absorbed in it, making himself unable to look at what was around him. In the same way, a certain theological current, which considers itself to be in continuity with the Greek Fathers and the Tradition of the early centuries in general, looks at itself in the mirror of the LXX as the source of apologetics and catechesis, so that "every attack on the LXX, in its *veritas graeca*, is an assault on the *veritas christiana*."[27] A position like this would look with suspicion on the last Augustine who, after years of discussion with Jerome, and on the basis of the information which he and Origen had introduced, elevated his gaze to open himself to a synthetic position which embraced that which "the Spirit of God did not intend to say through the latter [LXX interpreters], but through the former [Hebrew] prophets."[28]

Unlike the situation that existed at the turn of the fourth and fifth centuries C.E., during the polemic between Jerome and Augustine, today we have quite an exhaustive knowledge of the textual complexity of the OT and the richness of its different traditions, in addition to having available

---

26. In textual criticism, the project that is most similar to this trend is *The Hebrew Bible: A Critical Edition* (HBCE), which for the first time intends to make eclectic editions (not simply diplomatic ones with a critical apparatus at the bottom of the page, as done until now) of each book of the Hebrew Bible. For now a single volume has appeared: Fox, *Proverbs*. The general editor of the series, R. Hendel, describes the objective of this edition as follows: "The HBCE editions aim to restore, to the extent possible, the manuscript that was the latest common ancestor of all the extant witnesses. This earliest inferable text is called the archetype. The archetype is not identical to the original text (however one defines this elusive term) but is the earliest recoverable text of a particular book. To be more precise, the HBCE will approximate the corrected archetype, since the archetype, like all manuscripts, will have scribal errors that can be remedied" (Hendel, "Series Foreword," ix). Hendel presents this project as heir to the spirit of the Polyglot Bibles, though not in the sense of the valuing of the different textual traditions but rather in the sense of the availability of an ample amount of material which will serve the purpose of arriving at an eclectic text (cf. Hendel, "From Polyglot to Hypertext," 30–31). Cf. also Hendel, *Steps to a New Edition*.

27. "I Padri, anche se non nel *consensus omnium* e con le stesse modalità, scelgono Narciso, ovvero la tradizione come accumulo di conoscenze gerarchizzate e riflesse il cui processo autogenerativo è la fonte del progresso teologico-dogmatico. In questo orizzonte ogni attacco alla LXX, nella sua *veritas graeca*, è un attentato alla *veritas christiana*: un universo conoscitivo che si riconosce in un testo quale nutrimento autoritativo della sua apologia e catechesi" (Veltri, "L'ispirazione della LXX," 67–68).

28. Augustine, *Civ.* 18.43.

excellent historical studies and sufficient theological and hermeneutical reflection, to overcome the old diatribe without needing to eliminate or obviate either of its poles.

CHAPTER 10

The Synthetic Principle in the Liturgical Translations

I WILL CLOSE MY EXPOSITION by going back to one of the questions with which I began: On which text should our liturgical translations be based? The question, in the course of the review I have carried out, has become so full of content that it has become more than relevant, since the different textual traditions of a single book, or of one of its passages (or of a lone verse), can become very different.

A BIBLE WITH SEVERAL COLUMNS?

Now, the proposal for a Bible with several columns, with which I culminated the review above—does it not complicate the problem rather than resolving it? It is obvious that in our liturgy we cannot read the same passage from the prophet Jeremiah in three different versions (for example, three modern translations following, respectively, the MT, the LXX and a Qumran manuscript).

One possible solution would be to produce a "unified," eclectic text, not in the "vertical" or genealogical sense (the text which could be at the origin of the different textual traditions) but in the horizontal or synoptic sense: a broad text which receives all the differences in a kind of harmony (in the image of the harmonies of the gospels which gather in a single text all the information from the four). Nor would this solution be adequate. Many of the differences cannot be unified in a single version because, as we have already seen, we are not looking at accumulative accounts (in the image of the material peculiar to each evangelist) but at alternatives. Moreover, the result of such a large operation would be a text which has never existed and which, paradoxically, is not supported by any tradition.

Actually, the proposal for a Bible with several columns already contains within itself the answer to the question about which text to read in the liturgy. The columns refer to different traditions which involve not only a particular language, but also a particular liturgy and even a characteristic law. The Catholic-Latin tradition has for many centuries read the Bible in Latin, in its Vulgate form,[1] within a liturgy which is essentially of the Roman rite[2] and with a particular ecclesiastical law which is not universal. For its part, in the Orthodox or Catholic East, the Bible has been read in Greek since the beginning, within its own liturgy, which is different from the Western one, and also has an exclusive law. We could also speak of the Syriac churches, which, in spite of the centuries of Muslim domination, continue reading the Bible in Syriac, in the Peshitta version, with a liturgy and a law of their own.

The Bible with several columns would also embrace, in a way, the reading which the synagogue does of the Hebrew Bible (protocanonical books of the OT) according to the Masoretic tradition and vocalization, especially bearing in mind that the Latin churches depend, through the translation of Saint Jerome, on a Proto-Masoretic text which only the Jews have preserved.

In this way, the text to be read in the liturgy would be determined by the tradition to which each particular Church belongs. It would be a symphonic reading, on the basis of a polyglot score (Bible), in the image of the tetramorphic reading of the single gospel in the very first beats of its spread, when it is very likely that the most important churches read their own version (Matthew, Mark, Luke or John), while accepting the existence of the other three which were read in other churches.

---

1. With the exception of some areas, such as Hispania or North Africa, where the dominion of the *Vetus Latina* extended for centuries until it gave way to the Vulgate.

2. Before the Roman rite became prevalent as the dominant rite, other local rites existed which gradually died out or, as in the case of the Mozarabic, were reduced to a marginal status. Only the Ambrosian rite maintains an active presence in the diocese of Milan and its vicinity.

The Synthetic Principle in the Liturgical Translations

HOW SHOULD TRANSLATION FOR LITURGICAL READING BE DONE?

Bearing in mind that in the liturgy we read the Bible according to our own tradition, how is this reading affected by the synthetic principle to which I have referred in the last part of the exposition? To answer this question it is necessary to concentrate on a particular liturgical tradition to see how, in fact, that synthetic principle acts and, at the same time, how it could subsequently (as a *desideratum*) work. I will focus on the reading of the biblical text within the tradition of the Roman rite of the Catholic Church.

The biblical text which we read in the Roman liturgy follows the Neo-Vulgate *editio typica*,[3] so that the translations into vernacular languages for liturgical ends must be adapted to that particular Latin version. What is the Neo-Vulgate?[4] Perhaps it would be useful to begin by saying what it is *not*. We must not confuse this version with the two projects for a critical edition of the Vulgate which were completed in the final decades of the twentieth century. The first was an *editio critica maior*, published in several volumes, which the Benedictines began because of an assignment by Pius X in 1907 (starting in 1933 they congregated in the Pontifical Abbey of Saint Jerome-in-the-City, in Rome) and which they completed in 1995.[5] It was a rigorous work of collection and revision of the Latin manuscripts of the Vulgate in order to produce a critical edition using modern criteria. The second project has benefited partially from the progress of the first, although it has worked independently. It is conceived of as a manual edition or *editio critica minor*, in a single volume, with a reduced critical apparatus, and has been sponsored by the German Bible Society.[6]

The Neo-Vulgate, on the other hand, no longer includes the text of the Vulgate. It is a new Latin version done from the "original" texts of each book (Hebrew, Aramaic, Greek) which has made use of the translation of the Vulgate when it matched those texts. The Apostolic Constitution *Scripturarum Thesaurus*, by John Paul II, by which the first edition (1979) was promulgated, describes the nature and purposes of this initiative, which

---

3. *Nuova Vulgata Bibliorum Sacrorum*.

4. For a study of this version, cf. García Moreno, *Neovulgata*.

5. The series, edited by the Abbatia Pontificia Sancti Hieronymi in Urbe, bears the title *Biblia sacra iuxta latinam versionem ad codicum fidem*.

6. Weber and Gryson, *Biblia Sacra*.

was sponsored by Paul VI after the Second Vatican Council and which intended

> to revise all the books of Sacred Scripture so that the Church might be enriched with a Latin edition which advancing biblical studies demanded and which might serve especially in the Liturgy. In realizing this revision, "the old text of the Vulgate edition was taken into consideration word for word, namely, whenever the original texts are accurately rendered, such as they are found in modern critical editions; however the text was prudently improved, whenever it departs from them or interprets them less correctly."[7] . . . This New Vulgate edition will also be of such a nature that vernacular translations, which are destined for liturgical and pastoral use, may be referred to it.[8]

The result of this edition is a distinct departure from the old Vulgate because the latter is not its starting point but a "treasure" of expressions and vocabulary which, whenever they are accurately rendered, are preserved. The differences between the Vulgate and the Neo-Vulgate proceed from both the starting point and the mode of translating. With regard to the starting point, the Vulgate, in those books with a Hebrew original, had before it a Proto-Masoretic text. The Neo-Vulgate, on the other hand, starts with a modern critical edition of the Bible Hebrew, specifically the *Biblia Hebraica Stuttgartensia*, which includes a critical apparatus with the variants from the ancient versions, starting with the LXX, in addition to the testimony of some Qumran manuscripts (those which had already been published in the 1970s, when that critical edition was finished).[9] The translators of the Neo-Vulgate carried out a labor of textual criticism to arrive,

---

7. The quotation is from a speech by Paul VI (December 22, 1977).

8. EB 774.

9. The *Praenotanda* of the Neo-Vulgate specify fourteen passages in Isaiah in which the testimony of Qumran manuscripts 1QIs^a and 1QIs^b, alone or supported by other versions, is preferable (and determines the Latin translation chosen) to the reading of MT. The editors of the Neo-Vulgate have not been able to do this critical work on other books since the *Biblia Hebraica Stuttgartensia* contained in its apparatus only a very small part of the biblical witnesses from Qumran. Most of the editions of the biblical manuscripts from the Dead Sea were published between the years 1992 and 2010. The *Biblia Hebraica Quinta* (BHQ), in progress, is already collecting all the material from Qumran. By its very nature, the Neo-Vulgate, by linking itself to the critical edition of the Hebrew Bible (for the protocanonical books), should be looking at a new edition, on the basis of the BHQ, by following its pull toward the *hebraica veritas*.

The Synthetic Principle in the Liturgical Translations

with the help of the ancient witnesses, at an eclectic Hebrew text, which is in fact what we call the Pre-Masoretic text.[10]

With regard to the mode of translating, the Neo-Vulgate looks for a "precise" or "exact" mode of expression,[11] for which reason, with regard to the Latin terms themselves, it frequently departs from Jerome's translation, although the sense may not always vary too much. Obviously the advances in linguistic studies and comparative philology, which have enriched the dictionaries, make possible a greater understanding of the Hebrew text and, therefore, a translation which is more exact or faithful to the original.

In a certain way, the decision to do a new translation, thus departing from Jerome's version, merely highlights the principle of the *hebraica veritas* which the monk of Bethlehem upheld. Fidelity to this principle, within the Western tradition, has not crystalized in a single immovable version (the Vulgate), but by its nature has promoted a new translation which follows the advances in textual criticism which, over the course of time (including the discovery of new textual witnesses), has purified the "original" Hebrew text (the *hebraica veritas*). In earlier chapters I criticized Jerome's intention to identify the *hebraica veritas* with the Hebrew manuscripts with which the Jews of that time had provided him, that is, a Proto-Masoretic text. The Neo-Vulgate in some way overcomes that ingenuousness on the basis of a critical labor which takes us closer to the Hebrew text which is at the origin of the one with which the Dalmatian doctor was familiar, that is, the Pre-Masoretic text which could be placed around the second century B.C.E. in Palestine. Now, the identification of the Pre-Masoretic text with the "original" Hebrew text continues to be problematic, as we have seen throughout this study: this textual form coexisted in the second century B.C.E. with other forms, like the Pre-Samaritan (for the Pentateuch) and the Hebrew *Vorlage* of the LXX.

Together with the pull toward the *hebraica veritas*, the Neo-Vulgate, in this case like the Vulgate, accepts the other principle, the *Septuaginta auctoritas*, embracing in its canon the books which apostolic tradition, and later tradition, had received in what we call the Greek version of the LXX. Actually, this second principle does not just determine the canon of books that we read in the liturgy. In fact, it is in play in another series of translation

---

10. The same work is being done on the texts which Saint Jerome did not translate, on the basis of the critical editions of the Greek text that are preserved.

11. The Apostolic Constitution *Scripturarum Thesaurus* uses the Latin terms "accurate" and "recte" to describe the proper way to translate the Hebrew text (cf. EB 774).

decisions which permeate the Neo-Vulgate and find their expression in our liturgy in vernacular languages. Here is where we see in action the synthetic principle about which I have been talking. Below, I will describe with some examples how this principle works, in order to later set out a *desideratum* about a more extensive use of the principle in question.

Indeed, the general principle which leads to translating with precision and exactness from a critical edition of the Hebrew Bible (in the case of the protocanonical books), is not followed in isolated cases, precisely because another principle takes over: the Christian reception of the OT, both in the NT and in apostolic tradition. Here are some examples.

The Neo-Vulgate continues to translate the Hebrew term עלמה, "damsel," in Isa 7:14 as *virgo*, "virgin," which is certainly not a precise and exact translation of the Hebrew term but an acceptance of its translation in the LXX (παρθένος), which is taken in the gospel of Matthew (Matt 1:23) as a messianic prophecy which is fulfilled in the Virgin Mary. In the same way, the *tetragrammaton* or divine name (יהוה) is not transliterated (*yhwh*), nor is a vocalization of it attempted in order to reconstruct the original form (as the name *Yahweh* might be), but it is translated as *Dominus*, following a Jewish tradition which is reflected both in the MT (which by way of vocalization obliges it to be read 'adonay, "Lord") and in the LXX (Κύριος),[12] and which is received in the NT.

In the Psalms, the Neo-Vulgate does not follow the exception of the Vulgate (the *textus receptus* of which, as has been seen, is a translation of the Psalter *iuxta LXX*) but rather, following the general criterion, is based on the Hebrew text, and uses the Vulgate (the Gallican Psalter!) only when its terms are a good translation of the Hebrew.[13] However, in Ps 8:6, where the Hebrew text says "you have made him little less than a *God* (or 'the gods'; MT אלהים; Psalter *iuxta hebraicam veritatem*: *Deo*)," the Neo-Vulgate translates "you have made him little less than *the angels*" (*Minuisti eum paulo minus ab angelis*). In the interpretation of *'elohim* as "angels," the Neo-Vulgate follows a Jewish tradition attested by the LXX in Ps 8:6[14] and received by the NT in the letter to the Hebrews (Heb 2:5–9).

---

12. The same Jewish tradition continues in the Syriac Peshitta, which translates the Hebrew *tetragrammaton* as ܡܪܝܐ, "Lord."

13. In fact, it uses the numbering of the Psalms from the MT, while putting in parentheses that of the LXX (= Gallican Psalter).

14. Cf. this same tradition of interpretation in the reading of Ps 97:7 in LXX and Peshitta. The Syriac version expands this tradition to the appearance of *'elohim* in Ps 82:1; 89:7; 138:1 (in addition to 8:6). Cf. Carbajosa, *Character of the Syriac Version*, 146–50.

The Synthetic Principle in the Liturgical Translations

These examples seem to be based on one of the criteria, clarified in the *Praefatio ad lectorem* of the *editio typica altera* of the Neo-Vulgate, which guide the translation, namely, to respect the sense which the exegetical tradition of the Fathers or the Magisterium of the Church gave to the texts.[15] However, this same *Praefatio* turns out to be ambiguous when it encourages the avoidance of inserting doctrines from the NT into the translation of the OT, as well as "clarifications" from later tradition in the translation of the NT. This is a criterion which can be shared, provided that it means not inserting anything that is not in the manuscripts.[16] The problem is whether those manuscripts are only those of the Hebrew "original text" (*textus primigenius*, constantly cited in the *Praefatio* and the *Praenotanda*), and the variant readings of the ancient versions, especially those of the Septuagint accepted by the NT, are considered "clarifications" which should be avoided in order to return to the "primitive" text.[17] In some cases, the strong principle of the *hebraica veritas*, characteristic of Western tradition, runs the risk of leading, in the Neo-Vulgate, to the *pan-Hebraism* to which I have previously alluded.[18] However, the examples which I have given above show that, in fact, the criterion of translating according to the primitive text is found to be frequently corrected by the weight of a tradition expressed fundamentally in the LXX and in the reception of its readings in the NT. In this

---

15. "3. In vocabulis seligendis et in sensu textus primigenii Latine exprimendo, debito modo ratio habenda est etiam traditionis exegeticae sive Patrum sive Magisterii Ecclesiae, ita ut nova recensio Vulgatae fideliter reddat sensum 'quem tenuit et tenet sancta Mater Ecclesia'" (*Praefatio ad lectorem*, in *Nuova Vulgata Bibliorum Sacrorum*, 11).

16. "3. . . . Cavendum tamen omnino erit ne in vertendos textus Veteris Testamenti inferantur doctrinae Novi Testamenti; item ne in textus Novi Testamenti inducantur 'explicitationes' traditionis serioris. Ex altera tamen parte, versio singulorum textuum talis sit ut doctrina Novi Testamenti vel traditionis ecclesiasticae facile cum ea componi possit" (*Praefatio ad lectorem*, in *Nuova Vulgata Bibliorum Sacrorum*, 11).

17. "4. Ad 'explicitationes' quod attinet, quae sive in versione LXX Interpretum, sive in Vetere Latina, sive etiam apud s. Hieronymum haud raro inveniuntur, praesertim de Messianismo, in iis diiudicandis norma textus primigenii servetur, et versio ad regulam praecedentis commatis (n. 3) fiat. Semper autem caveatur ne libro alicui vel aetati plus tribuatur quam quod revera habuit, ita ut germanus progressus revelationis perspiciatur. Quod si agatur de textibus, qui decursu temporum realem progressionem habuerunt, in iis vertendis ea vocabula seligantur quae eiusmodi progressioni excipiendae sint apta" (*Praefatio ad lectorem*, in *Nuova Vulgata Bibliorum Sacrorum*, 11).

18. The labors of the commission in charge of the new Latin translation extend from 1965 to 1977, a time in which the textual criticism of the OT tended to use the ancient versions exclusively as a resource for reconstructing an "original" Hebrew text.

way, the synthetic principle of which I have been speaking permeates the Latin *editio typica* on which our modern liturgical translations are based.

A CONCLUDING DESIDERATUM

The *desideratum* with which I want to conclude this study has to do with the application of the synthetic principle in question when translating certain texts from the OT in a liturgical context, especially when passages from the OT and the NT are read in a linked form. This context is especially clear in the liturgy of the word within the eucharistic celebration, in which the text of the OT has a thematic unity with the gospel, especially on Sundays. The *Order of Readings for Mass* (Latin *Ordo Lectionum Missae* [*OLM*]), which is printed in the Lectionaries as the *General Introduction*, says the following:

> The present Order of Readings selects Old Testament texts mainly because of their correlation with New Testament texts read in the same Mass, and particularly with the gospel text. (*OLM*, 67)

In some cases one does not find that the "correlation" between the texts selected from the OT and NT is accompanied by a textual "correlation," that is, that the textual form of the OT which is received by the NT is that which is presented in the liturgy.

I will give an example which has to do with a text that has already been studied: Psalm 40 (39) and it relationship with the letter to the Hebrews. On the Tuesday of the third week of Ordinary Time (year I), the liturgy of the word in the Eucharist gives us as the first reading Heb 10:1–10. The central passage of that reading (Heb 10:5–7) reads as follows in the Catholic liturgical tradition (following the Neo-Vulgate):

> For this reason, when he came into the world, he said: Sacrifice and offering you did not desire, *but a body you prepared for me*; in burnt offerings and sin offerings you took no delight. Then I said, As is written of me in the scroll, Behold, I come to do your will, O God.

With much intelligence, we are given as the response of the people to this reading Psalm 40, which is precisely the one which the author of the letter to the Hebrews is quoting and which is put into the mouth of the Son when he enters the world, in dialogue with the Father. The lectionary has the people repeat, as a refrain, the phrase "Here am I, Lord, I come to do your will," while a psalmist recites the verses of the Psalm, following the

The Synthetic Principle in the Liturgical Translations

liturgical translation, until he comes to the verses (Ps 40:7–8) which make up the heart of the dialogue of the Word with the Father:

> Sacrifice or oblation you wished not,
> but ears open to obedience you gave me.
> Burnt offerings or sin-offerings you sought not;
> then said I, "Behold I come."

The Psalmist, before the assembly, has "corrected" Christ himself by changing the words of his filial conversation. The obedience of the Son is no longer that of accepting the body which the Father has given him but that of accepting that his ear be opened (in a sign of submission). In a case like this it is strange that the Neo-Vulgate does not follow the version of the LXX, which is the one quoted by the letter to the Hebrews, as it follows the quoted Greek version in Isa 7:14 (by choosing *virgo*) in order to facilitate "consistency" with the gospel de Matthew.

It is worthwhile to extend the synthetic principle, which frequently guides our translations, to cover paradigmatic texts like the one mentioned above, especially when, in the liturgical context which expresses our faith, the OT and NT enter into dialogue. It is then that there is shown the fruitfulness of combining, and not setting against one another, the two principles in dispute, *hebraica veritas et Septuaginta auctoritas*.

Bibliography

Abbatia Pontificia Sancti Hieronymi in Urbe. *Biblia sacra iuxta latinam versionem ad codicum fidem.* Rome: Typis Polyglottis Vaticanis, 1926–95.

Amara, Dalia. "Daniel. Septuagint." In *THB* 1C 542–54.

Attridge, Harold W., and Margot E. Fassler, eds. *Psalms in Community: Jewish and Christian Textual, Liturgical, and Artistic Traditions.* Society of Biblical Literature Symposium Series 25. Atlanta: SBL, 2003.

Auvray, Paul. "Comment se pose le problème de l'inspiration des Septante." *Revue Biblique* 59 (1952) 321–36.

Bagnall, Roger S. *Early Christian Books in Egypt.* Princeton: Princeton University Press, 2009.

Barthélemy, Dominique. "L'Ancien Testament a mûri à Alexandrie." *Theologische Zeitschrift* 21 (1965) 358–70.

———. *Les Devanciers d'Aquila.* Leiden: Brill, 1963.

———. "Origène et le texte de l'Ancien Testament." In *Epektasis, Mélanges patristiques offerts au Cardinal Jean Daniélou*, edited by Jacques Fontaine and Charles Kannengiesserl, 247–61. Paris: Beauchesne, 1972.

———. "La place de la Septante dans l'Église." In *Aux grands carrefours de la révélation et de l'exégèse de l'Ancien Testament*, edited by Charles Hauret, 13–28. Paris: Desclée de Brower, 1967.

———. "Redécouverte d'un chaînon manquant de l'histoire de la Septante." *Revue Biblique* 60 (1953) 18–29.

Beentjes, Pancratius C., ed. *The Book of Ben Sira in Modern Research.* Berlin: de Gruyter, 1997.

Belli, Filippo, et al. *Vetus in Novo: El recurso a la Escritura en el Nuevo Testamento.* Madrid: Encuentro, 2006.

Benoit, Pierre. "L'inspiration des Septante d'après les Pères." In *L'Homme devant Dieu, mélanges offerts au Père Henri De Lubac.* Vol 1, *Exégèse et Patristique*, 169–87. Paris: Aubier, 1963.

———. "La Septante est-elle inspirée?" In *Vom Wort des Lebens: Festschrift für Max Meinertz*, edited by Nikolaus Adler, 41–49. Münster: Aschendorff, 1951.

Berger, Samuel. *Histoire de la Vulgate pendant les premiers siècles du Moyen Âge.* Paris: Berger-Levrault, 1893.

Bertram, Georg. "Praeparatio evangelica in der Septuaginta." *Vetus Testamentum* 7 (1957) 225–49.

Bible de Jérusalem. Paris: du Cerf, 1961.

Bibliography

Black, Matthew, and William A. Smalley, eds. *On Language, Culture, and Religion: In Honor of Eugene A. Nida*. La Haye: Mouton, 1974.

Blanchard, Alain, ed. *Les débuts du codex*. Turnhout: Brepols, 1989.

Boers, Hendrikus. W. "Psalm 16 and the Historical Origin of the Christian Faith." *Zeitschrift für die alttestamentliche Wissenschaft* 60 (1969) 105–10.

Bogaert, Pierre-Maurice. "Job latin chez les Pères et dans les Bibles: D'une version courte à des versions longues sur le grec et sur l'hébreu." *Revue Bénédictine* 122 (2012) 48–99, 366–93.

Boyd-Taylor, Cameron. "The Semantics of Biblical Language Redux." In *"Translation Is Required": The Septuagint in Retrospect and Prospect*, edited by Robert J. V. Hiebert, 41–57. Atlanta: SBL, 2010.

Brock, Sebastian P. "Greek into Syriac and Syriac into Greek." *Journal of the Syriac Academy* 3 (1977) 1–17.

———. "The Syriac Orient: A Third 'Lung' for the Church?" *Orientalia Christiana Periodica* 71 (2005) 5–20.

Brooke, Alan England et al., eds. *The Old Testament in Greek: According to the Text of Codex Vaticanus, Supplemented from Other Uncial Manuscripts, with a Critical Apparatus Containing the Variants of the Chief Ancient Authorities for the Text of the Septuagint*. Cambridge: Cambridge University Press, 1906.

Brown, Raymond E. *An Introduction to the New Testament*. New York: Doubleday, 1997.

Buzzetti, Carlo. "Traduzione della Bibbia e ispirazione della LXX." *Rivista Biblica* 20 (1972) 153–61.

Bynum, W. Randolf. *The Fourth Gospel and the Scriptures: Illuminating the Form and Meaning of Scriptural Citation in John 19:37*. Leiden: Brill, 2012.

Cañas Reíllo, José Manuel. "Daniel: Vetus Latina." In *THB* 1C 575–78.

Carbajosa, Ignacio. "A los 500 años de la Biblia Políglota Complutense: Enseñanzas de un gran proyecto editorial." In *Una Biblia a varias voces: Estudio textual de la Biblia Políglota Complutense*, edited by Ignacio Carbajosa and Andrés García Serrano, 15–42. Madrid: Ediciones Universidad San Dámaso, 2014.

———. *The Character of the Syriac Version of Psalms: A Study of Psalms 90–150 in the Peshitta*. Translated by Paul Stevenson. Leiden: Brill, 2008.

———. *Faith, the Fount of Exegesis: The Interpretation of Scripture in Light of the History of Research on the Old Testament*. Translated by Paul Stevenson. San Francisco: Ignatius, 2013.

———. "Peshitta." In *THB* 1A 262–78.

———. "The Syriac Old Testament Tradition: Moving from Jerusalem to Athens." In *Eastern Crossroads: Essays on Medieval Christian Legacy*, edited by in Juan Pedro Monferrer-Sala, 109–30. Piscataway, NJ: Gorgias, 2007.

———. "La vida de los manuscritos bíblicos: Cuando la tradición de lectura se hace Escritura." *Estudios Bíblicos* 71 (2013) 169–99.

Carbajosa, Ignacio, and Andrés García Serrano, eds. *Una Biblia a varias voces: Estudio textual de la Biblia Políglota Complutense*. Madrid: Ediciones Universidad San Dámaso, 2014.

Childs, Brevard S. "Psalm 8 in the Context of the Christian Canon." *Interpretation* 23 (1969) 20–31.

Cimosa, Mario "La traduzione greca dei LXX: Dibattito sull'ispirazione." *Salesianum* 46 (1984) 3–14.

Bibliography

Cox, Claude. "Does a Shorter Hebrew Parent Text Underlie Old Greek Job?" In *In the Footsteps of Sherlock Holmes: Studies in the Biblical Text in Honour of Anneli Aejmelaeus*, edited by Timothy M. Law et al., 451–62. Leuven: Peeters, 2014.

———. "Job. Septuagint." In *THB* 1C 175–81.

Crawford, Sidnie W., et al. "Sample Editions of the Oxford Hebrew Bible: Deuteronomy 32:1–9, 1 Kings 11:1–8, and Jeremiah 27:1–10 (34 G)." *Vetus Testamentum* 58 (2008) 352–66.

Dodd, Charles H. *According to the Scriptures: The Sub-structure of New Testament Theology*. London: Nisbet, 1952.

Dreyfus, François. "L'inspiration de la Septante: Quelques difficultés à surmonter." *Revue des sciences philosophiques et théologiques* 49 (1965) 210–20.

Drijvers, Han J. W. *The Book of the Laws of Countries: Dialogue on Fate of Bardaisan of Edessa*. Assen: Van Gorcum, 1965.

———. "Syrian Christianity and Judaism." In *The Jews among the Pagans and Christians: In the Roman Empire*, edited by Judith Lieu et al., 124–46. London: Routledge, 1992.

Dubarle, André-Marie. "Note conjointe sur l'inspiration de la Septante." *Revue des sciences philosophiques et théologiques* 49 (1965) 221–29.

Feder, Frank. "Job. Coptic Translations." In *THB* 1C 209–11.

Fernández Marcos, Natalio. *Septuaginta: la biblia griega de judíos y cristianos*. Salamanca: Sígueme, 2008.

Fischer, Bonifatius. *Lateinische Bibelhandschriften im frühen Mittelalter*. Freiburg: Herder, 1985.

Foster, Lewis A. "The 'Q' Myth in Synoptic Studies." *Bulletin of the Evangelical Theological Society* 7 (1964) 111–19.

Fox, Michael V. *Proverbs: An Eclectic Edition with Introduction and Commentary*. Atlanta: SBL, 2015.

Francis. *Scripturae Sacrae Affectus*. https://www.vatican.va/content/francesco/en/apost_letters/documents/papa-francesco-lettera-ap_20200930_scripturae-sacrae-affectus.html.

Gamble, Harry Y. *Books and Readers in the Early Church: A History of Early Christian Texts*. New Haven: Yale University Press, 1995.

García Moreno, Antonio. *La Neovulgata: Precedentes y actualidad*. Pamplona: Eunsa, 1986.

General Council of Trent. *Fourth Session*. https://www.papalencyclicals.net/councils/trent/fourth-session.htm.

Gentry, Peter. "Pre-Hexaplaric Translations, Hexapla, post-Hexaplaric Translations." In *THB* 1A 211–35.

———. "'The Role of the "Three" in the Text History of the Septuagint': II. Aspects of Interdependence of the Old Greek and the Three in Ecclesiastes." *Aramaic Bible* 4 (2006) 153–92.

Gorea, Maria. *Job repensé ou trahi? Omissions et raccourcis de la Septante*. Paris: Gabalda, 2007.

Grelot, Pierre. *Le Mystère du Christ dans le Psaumes*. Paris: Desclée de Brouwer, 1998.

———. "Sur l'inspiration et la canonicité de la Septante." *Science ecclésiastiques* 16 (1964) 387–418.

———. "Le texte du Psaume 39,7 dans la Septante." *Revue Biblique* 108 (2001) 210–13.

Gzella, Holger. "New Ways in Textual Criticism: Isa 42,1–4 as a Paradigm Case." *Ephemerides Theologicae Lovanienses* 81 (2005) 387–423.

Bibliography

Hanhart, Robert "Die Bedeutung der Septuaginta in neutestamentlicher Zeit." *Zeitschrift für Theologie und Kirche* (1984) 395–416.

Hatch, Edwin. *Essays in Biblical Greek*. Oxford: Clarendon, 1889.

Hay, David M. *Glory at the Right Hand: Psalm 110 in Early Christianity*. Nashville: Abingdon, 1973.

Hendel, Ronald. "From Polyglot to Hypertext." In *THBE* 19–33.

———. *Steps to a New Edition of the Hebrew Bible*. Atlantqa: SBL, 2016.

Hengel, Martin *The Septuagint as Christian Scripture: Its Prehistory and the Problem of Its Canon*. London: T. & T. Clark, 2002.

Hübner, Hans. *Vetus Testamentum in Novo*. 2 vols. Göttingen: Vandenhoeck & Ruprecht, 1997–2005.

Hurtado, Larry W. *The Earliest Christians Artifacts: Manuscripts and Christian Origins*. Grand Rapids: Eerdmans, 2006.

Jenkins, R. G. "Colophons of the Syrohexapla and the *Textgeschichte* of the Recensions of Origen." In *VII Congress of the International Organization for Septuagint and Cognate Studies, Leuven 1989*, edited by Claude E. Cox, 261–77. Atlanta: Scholars, 1991.

———. "Hexaplaric Marginalia and the Hexapla-Tetrapla Question." In *Origen's Hexapla and Fragments*, edited by Alison Salvesen, 73–87. Tübingen: Mohr Siebeck, 1998.

Jerome. *Epistolario: Edición bilingüe: Traducción, introducciones y notas de Juan Bautista Valero*. 2 vols. Madrid: BAC, 1993–95.

———. *Obras Completas de San Jerónimo: Edición bilingüe promovida por la orden de San Jerónimo*. 15 vols. Madrid: BAC, 1999–2015.

The Jerusalem Bible. London: Darton, Longman, & Todd 1966.

Jódar, Carlos. "Is 6,9–10 en el Nuevo Testamento." In *Vetus in Novo: El recurso a la Escritura en el Nuevo Testamento*, edited by Filippo Belli et al., 102–29. Madrid: Encuentro, 2006.

Johnson, Allan Chester, et al. *The John H. Scheide Biblical Papyri: Ezekiel*. Princeton: Princeton University Press, 1938.

Joosten, Jan. "The Old Testament Quotations in the Old Syriac and Peshitta Gospels: A Contribution to the Study of the Diatessaron." *Textus* 15 (1990) 55–76.

Jouassard, Georges. "Réflexions sur la position de saint Augustin relativement aux Septante dans sa discussion avec saint Jérôme." *Revue des études augustiniennes* 2 (1956) 93–99.

Juel, Donald. "Social Dimensions of Exegesis: The Use of Psalm 16 in Acts 2." *Catholic Biblical Quarterly* 43 (1981) 543–56.

Karrer, Martin. "The Septuagint Text in Early Christianity." In *Introduction to the Septuagint*, edited by Siegfried Kreuzer, 613–26. Waco, TX: Baylor University Press, 2019.

Kilgallen, John J. "The Use of Psalm 16:8–11 in Peter's Pentecost Speech." *Expository Times* 113 (2001) 47–50.

Kirk, Geoffrey S. "Aristarchus and the Scholia." In *The Iliad: A Commentary*. Vol. 1, *Books 1–4*, edited by Geoffrey S. Kirk, 38–43. Cambridge: Cambridge University Press, 1985.

Klein, Hans. "Zur Wirkungsgeschichte von Psalm 8." In *Konsequente Traditionsgeschichte: Festschrift für Klaus Baltzer Zum 65. Geburtstag*, edited by Rüdiger Bartelmus et al., 183–98. Gottingen: Vandenhoeck & Ruprecht, 1993.

Kooij, Arie van der. "Compositions and Editions in Early Judaism: The Case of Daniel." In *THBE* 428–48.

Bibliography

———. "'The Servant of the Lord': A Particular Group of Jews in Egypt according to the Old Greek of Isaiah." In *Studies in the Book of Isaiah: Festschrift Willem A. M. Beuken*, edited by Jacques van Ruiten and Marc Vervenne, 383–96. Leuven: Peeters, 1997.

Kraus, Wolfgang. "The Significance of Septuagint Quotations in the New Testament against the Background of Old Testament Textual History." In *Introduction to the Septuagint*, edited by Siegfried Kreuzer, 627–40. Waco, TX: Baylor University Press, 2019.

La Bonnardière, Anne-Marie. "Augustin a-t-il utilisé la 'Vulgate' de Jérome?" In *Saint Augustin et la Bible*, edited by Anne-Marie la Bonnardière, 303–12. Paris: Beauchesne, 1986.

Law, Timothy M. "Origen's Parallel Bible: Textual Criticism, Apologetics, or Exegesis?" *Journal of Theological Studies* 59 (2008) 1–21.

———. *When God Spoke Greek: The Septuagint and the Making of the Christian Bible*. Oxford: Oxford University Press, 2013.

Letter of Aristeas. In *The Old Testament Pseudepigrapha*, edited by James H. Charlesworth, translated by R. J. H. Shutt, 2:7–34. London: Darton, Longman, & Todd, 1985.

Littman, Robert J. "Textual History of Tobit." In *THB* 2C 385–400.

Loader, William R. G. "Christ at the Right Hand: Ps CX.1 in the New Testament." *New Testament Studies* 24 (1978) 199–217.

Loewe, Raphael. "The Medieval History of the Latin Vulgate." In *The Cambridge History of the Bible*. Vol. 2, *The West from the Fathers to the Reformation*, edited by G. W. H. Lampe, 102–54. Cambridge: Cambridge University Press, 1969.

Lust, John. "Textual Criticism of the Old Testament and of the New Testament: Stepbrothers?" In *New Testament Textual Criticism and Exegesis: Festschrift Joël Delobel*, edited by Adelbert Denaux, 15–31. Leuven: Peeters, 2002.

Marrou, Henri-Irenee. *Saint Augustin et la fin de la culture Antique: "Retractacio."* Paris: Boccard, 1949.

———. *Saint Augustin et la fin de la culture Antique*. Paris: Boccard, 1938.

Martín Contreras, Elvira, and Guadalupe Seijas de los Ríos. *Masora: La transmisión de la tradición de la Biblia Hebrea*. Estella: Verbo Divino, 2010.

McLay, R. Timothy. *The Use of the Septuagint in New Testament Research*. Grand Rapids: Eerdmans, 2003.

Menken, Maarten J. J. *Matthew's Bible: The Old Testament Text of the Evangelist*. Leuven: Leuven University Press, 2004.

———. "The Textual Form and the Meaning of the Quotation from Zechariah 12:10 in John 19:37." *Catholic Biblical Quarterly* 55 (1993) 494–511.

———. "The Textual Form of the Quotation from Isaiah 7,14 in Matthew 1,23." *Novum Testamentum* 43 (2001) 144–60.

Mercati, Giuseppe. "Il problema della colonna II dell'Esaplo." *Biblica* 28 (1947) 1–30, 173–215.

———. *Psalterii Hexapli reliquiae: Pars Prima: Codex rescriptus Bybliothecae Ambrosianae O 39 sup. phototypice expressus et transcriptus*. Rome: Bybliotheca Vaticana, 1958.

Merx, Adalbert. *Bardesanes von Edessa: Nebst einer Untersuchung über das Verhältniss der clementinischen Recognitionem zu dem Buche der Gesetze der Länder*. Halle: Pfeffer, 1863.

Michel, Albert. *Les décrets du Concile de Trente*. Paris: Letouzey et Ané, 1938.

Morla, Víctor. *Los manuscritos hebreos de Ben Sira: Traducción y notas*. Estella: Verbo divino, 2012.

Bibliography

Moyise, Steve, and Maarten J. J. Menken, eds. *The Psalms in the New Testament*. London: T. & T. Clark, 2004.

Müller, Møgens. *The First Bible of the Church: A Plea for the Septuagint*. Sheffield: Sheffield Academic, 1996.

Muñoz Iglesias, Salvador. "El decreto tridentino sobre la Vulgata y su interpretación por los teólogos del siglo XVI." *Estudios Bíblicos* 5 (1946) 137–69.

Newman, Hillel I. "How Should We Measure Jerome's Hebrew Competence?" In *Jerome of Stridon: His Life, Writings, and Legacy*, edited by Andrew Cain and Josef Lössl, 131–40. Burlington, VT: Ashgate, 2009.

Nongbri, Brent. *God's Library: The Archeology of the Earliest Christian Manuscripts*. New Haven: Yale University Press, 2018.

Norton, Gerard J. "Observations on the First Two Columns of the Hexapla." In *Origen's Hexapla and Fragments*, edited by Aliaason Salvesen, 103–24. Tübingen: Mohr Siebeck, 1998.

Nuova Vulgata Bibliorum Sacrorum. Rome: Editrice Vaticana, 1986.

Origen. *Sur les écritures: Philocalie, 1–20*. Translated by Nicholas de Lange. Sources Chrétiennes 302. Paris: du Cerf, 1983.

Peña, Ignacio. "San Jerónimo en el desierto de Calcis (años 375–377)." *Studia Orientalia Christiana. Collectanea* 19 (1986) 285–300.

Petersen, William L. *Tatian's Diatessaron: Its Creation, Dissemination, Significance, and History in Scholarship*. Leiden: Brill, 1994.

Piquer Otero, Andrés, and Pablo Torijano Morales. "מלכים, Βασιλειῶν, Reges: Textual Plurality as a Constellation Cluster and the Challenge of Editing a Star-Map." In *THBE* 347–69.

Rahlfs, Alfred, and Robert Hanhart, eds. *Septuaginta*. Stuttgart: German Bible Society, 2006.

Roberts, Colin H., and Theodore C. Skeat. *The Birth of the Codex*. Oxford: Oxford University Press, 1983.

Rüsen-Weinhold, Ulrich. *Der Septuagintapsalter im Neuen Testament: Eine textgeschichtliche Untersuchung*. Neukirchen-Vluyn: Neukirchener, 2004.

Schenker, Adrian "L'Ècriture sainte subsiste en plusieurs formes canoniques simultanées." In *L'Interpretazione della Bibbia nella Chiesa: Atti del Simposio promosso dalla Congregazione per la Dottrina della Fede: Roma, settembre 1999*, edited by Prosper Grech et al., 178–86. Vatican City: Editrice Vaticana, 2001.

Second Vatican Council. *Dei Verbum*. https://www.vatican.va/archive/hist_councils/ii_vatican_council/documents/vat-ii_const_19651118_dei-verbum_en.html.

Segal, Michael. "Daniel 5 in Aramaic and Greek and the Textual History of Daniel." In *Congress Volume Stellenbosch 2016*, edited by Louis C. Jonker et al., 251–84. Leiden: Brill 2017.

———. "The Old Greek Version and Masoretic Text of Daniel 6." In *Die Septuaginta: Orte und Intentionen*, edited by Siegfried Kreuzer et al., 404–28. Tübingen: Mohr Siebeck, 2016.

Septuaginta: Vetus Testamentum Graecum. Auctoritate Academiae Litteratum Gottingensis editum. 25 vols. Göttingen: Vandenhoeck & Ruprecht, 1931–.

Sgherri, Giuseppe. "Sulla valutazione origeniana dei LXX." *Biblica* 58 (1977) 1–28.

Shedinger, Robert F. "Did Tatian Use the Old Testament Peshitta? A Response to Jan Joosten." *Novum Testamentum* 41 (1999) 265–79.

Bibliography

Siegert, Folker. "La Bible des premiers chrétiens." *Annali di Storia dell'Esegesi* 22 (2005) 409–19.
Steyn, Gert J. *A Quest for the Assumed LXX Vorlage of the Explicit Quotations in Hebrews*. Göttingen: Vandenhoeck & Ruprecht, 2011.
Taylor, Charles. *Hebrew-Greek Cairo Genizah Palimpsest from the Taylor-Schechter Collection*. Cambridge: Cambridge University Press, 1900.
Toloni, Giancarlo. *L'originale del libro di Tobia: Studio filologico-linguistico*. Madrid: CSIC, 2004.
Tönges, Elke. "The Epistle to the Hebrews as a 'Jesus-Midrash.'" In *Hebrews: Contemporary Methods—New Insights*, edited by Gabriella Gelardini, 89–105. Leiden: Brill, 2005.
Tov, Emanuel. "Electronic Scripture Editions (With an Appendix Listing Electronic Editions on the Internet [2014])." In *THBE* 86–104.
———. "Hebrew Scripture Editions: Philosophy and Praxis." In *From 4QMMT to Resurrection: Mélanges qumraniens en hommage à Émile Puech*, edited by Florentino García Martínez et al., 281–312. Leiden: Brill, 2006.
———. "The Literary History of the Book of Jeremiah in the Light of Its Textual History." In *Empirical Models for Biblical Criticism*, edited by Jeffrey H. Tigay, 211–37. Philadelphia: University of Pennsylvania Press, 1985.
———. "The Nature of the Large-Scale Differences between the LXX and MT S T V, Compared with Similar Evidence in Other Sources." In *The Earliest Text of the Hebrew Bible: The Relationship between the Masoretic Text and the Hebrew Base of the Septuagint Reconsidered*, edited by Adrian Schenker, 121–43. Atlanta: SBL, 2003.
———. "The Rabbinic Tradition concerning the 'Alterations' Inserted into the Greek Translation of the Torah and Their Relation to the Original Text of the LXX." *Journal for the Study of Judaism* 15 (1984) 65–89.
Trapè, Agostino. *Agostino: L'uomo, il pastore, il mistico*. Rome: Città Nuova, 2001.
———. "Introduzione Generale: I. Teologia." In *Opere di Sant'Agostino: V. La Città di Dio: I. Libri I–X*, ix–xcviii. Rome: Città Nuova, 1990.
Troyer, Kristin de. "The Textual Plurality of the Book of Joshua and the Need for a Digital Complutensian Polyglot Bible." In *THBE* 330–46.
———. *The Ultimate and the Penultimate Text of the Book of Joshua*. Leuven: Peeters, 2018.
Urassa, Wenceslaus M. *Psalm 8 and Its Christological Re-interpretations in the New Testament Context: An Inter-contextual Study of Biblical Hermeneutics*. Frankfurt: Lang, 1998.
Vaccari, Alberto. "Esaple ed esaplare in S. Girolamo." *Biblica* 8 (1927) 463–68.
Veltri, Giuseppe. "L'ispirazione della LXX tra leggenda e teologia: Dal racconto di Aristea alla 'veritas hebraica' di Girolamo." *Laurentianum* 27 (1986) 3–71.
Wagner, J. Ross. *Heralds of the Good News: Isaiah and Paul "In Concert" in the Letter to the Romans*. Leiden: Brill, 2002.
———. "The Septuagint and the 'Search for the Christian Bible.'" In *Scripture's Doctrine and Theology's Bible: How the New Testament Shapes Christian Dogmatics*, edited by Markus Bockmuehl and Alan J. Torrance, 17–28. Grand Rapids: Baker Academic, 2008.
Wasserstein, Abraham, and David J. Wasserstein. *The Legend of the Septuagint: From Classical to Today*. Cambridge: Cambridge University Press, 2006.
Weber, Robert, and Roger Gryson, eds. *Biblia Sacra iuxta Vulgatam Versionem*. Stuttgart: Deutsche Bibelgesellschaft, 2007.

Weis, Richard D. "Jeremiah amid Actual and Virtual Editions: Textual Plurality and the Editing of the Book of Jeremiah." In *THBE* 370–99.
Wright, Benjamin G. "Textual History of Ben Sira." In *THB* 2B 187–98.
Ziegler, Joseph. "Die Bedeutung der Chester Beatty-Scheide Papyrus 967 für die Textüberlieferung der Ezechiel-Septuaginta." *Zeitschrift für die alttestamentliche Wissenschaft* 61 (1945–48) 74–96.

Author Index

Africanus, Julius, 50–52, 99
Akiva, Rabbi, 77
Alcuin of York, 88–90
Amara, Dalia, 15
Ambrose, Saint, 57
Aphrahat, 66
Aquila, 2, 7, 10, 19–22, 41, 49, 53, 55, 69, 77
Arias Montano, Benito, 97
Aristarchus of Samothrace, 19
Aristeas, 34–35, 42, 44, 59–60, 63, 73–76
Attridge, Harold W., 91
Augustine, Saint
   Hebrew text, 44, 47–48, 94–95, 99
   Hexapla, 5, 23, 94–96
   Inspiration, 59–60, 73–74, 94
   Letters to Jerome, 4–8, 23–24, 42, 44–45, 86, 95
   Septuagint, 12, 23–25, 42–45, 47–48, 59, 67, 74, 94–95, 99
   Septuaginta auctoritas, viii, xvi, 25, 32, 42–43, 53, 67, 94
   Vetus Latina, 8, 43
   Vulgate, 43–44, 51, 94
Auvray, Paul, 60–63

Bagnall, Roger S., 71
Bar Kokhba, 37
Baranina, Rabbi, 3, 22
Bardaisan of Edessa, 66
Barthélemy, Dominique, 7, 19, 21, 32, 45–46, 51–52, 56–58, 60, 66, 68, 75, 77, 95, 98
Beentjes, Pancratius C., 17
Benedict XVI, Pope, 58
Benoit, Pierre, 60–61, 63–64, 78–79

Berger, Samuel, 87
Bertram, Georg, 47
Blanchard, Alain, 71
Boers, Hendrikus, 91
Bogaert, Pierre-Maurice, 14
Bonnardière, Anne-Marie la, 44
Boyd-Taylor, Cameron, 58
Brock, Sebastian P., 66–67
Brooke, Alan England, 71
Brown, Raymond E., 96
Buzzetti, Carlo, 61
Bynum, W. Randolf, 68

Cañas Reíllo, José Manuel, 16
Cassiodorus of Squillace, 88
Carbajosa, Ignacio, 56, 66–67, 96–97, 99, 110
Charlemagne, Emperor, 87–88, 90
Childs, Brevard S., 91
Chrysostom, John, 63–64, 79
Cimosa, Mario, 61
Cisneros, Cardenal, 83, 96
Clement of Alexandria, 47
Cox, Claude, 14,
Crawford, Sidnie W., 98
Cyprian of Cartahge, 14, 16

Damasus, Pope, 1–2, 8, 43, 81, 86
Demetrius, 74
Dodd, Charles H., 91
Dreyfus, François, 60, 75–77
Drijvers, Han J. W., 66–67
Dubarle, André-Marie, 60, 75

Eleazar, High Priest, 43
Ephrem, Saint 66
Epiphanius of Salamis, 7

Author Index

Eusebius of Caesarea, 2, 20, 47
Exuperius, Bishop of Toulouse, 81
Ezra, 53, 55, 58, 64, 72, 79

Fassler, Margot E., 91
Feder, Frank, 14
Fernández Marcos, Natalio, 65
Francis, Pope, xv
Fischer, Bonifatius, 87–89
Foster, Lewis A., 96
Fox, Michael V., 103
Fretela, 22

Gamble, Harry Y., 71
García Moreno, Antonio, 107
García Serrano, Andrés, 96, 99
Gentry, Peter, 7, 22
Gorea, Maria, 13–14,
Gregory of Tours, 89–90
Grelot, Pierre, 50, 60, 62–63, 75–76, 78, 91
Gryson, Roger, 107
Gzella, Holger, 73

Hanhart, Robert, 68, 71
Hatch, Edwin, 14
Hay, David M., 91
Hendel, Ronald, 97, 103
Hesychius, 2, 7, 28
Hilary of Poitiers, 53–56, 58, 72
Hillel, 57, 77
Homer, 19
Hübner, Hans, 39
Hurtado, Larry W., 71

Innocent I, Pope, 81
Irenaeus, Saint, 21, 41, 53–55, 58, 71–72, 75

Jenkins, R. G., 20
Jerome, Saint,
  Canon, 16, 26, 51
  Hebraica veritas, viii, xvi, 3, 25–32, 35–37, 41, 84, 109
  Hebrew text, 8, 22, 25, 27–34, 36–41, 46, 67–69, 91, 94, 99, 109
  Hexapla, vii, 2, 20–22, 27–30, 51, 85, 94, 96

  Inspiration, 34–35, 63
  Letters to Augustine, 7, 95
  Life, 1–3,
  Septuagint, 15, 22, 24, 27–41, 46, 89, 99
  Vetus Latina, 2–3, 14, 30, 78, 85, 91
  Vulgate, xv, 1–4, 18, 22, 28, 31, 38, 40–41, 51, 82, 84–85, 87–89, 91, 94, 109
Jódar, Carlos, 40
John Paul II, Pope, 107
Johnson, Allan Chester, 13
Jonathan ben Uzziel, 77
Joosten, Jan, 66
Josephus, Flavius 35, 102
Josiah, King, 58, 72
Jouassard, Georges, 25
Juel, Donald, 91
Justin, Saint, 21, 41, 47, 71

Karrer, Martin, 49, 68
Kilgallen, John J., 91
Kirk, Geoffrey S., 19
Kittel, Rudolf, 97
Klein, Hans, 91
Kooij, Arie van der, 15, 73
Kraus, Wolfgang, 40, 46

Lange, Nicholas de, 50
Law, Timothy M., 19, 65–66, 102
Leo III, Pope, 87
Littman, Robert J., 18
Loader, William R. G., 91
Loewe, Raphael, 82, 87–88, 90
Lucian, 2, 7, 28
Lucifer of Cagliari, 14
Lust, John, 13

Marcela, 30
Marrou, Henri-Irenee, 23
Martín Contreras, Elvira, 86
Maurdramnus, Abbot of Corbie, 88
McLay, R. Timothy, 46
Menken, Maarten J. J., 40, 69–70, 91
Mercati, Giuseppe, 20, 22–23
Merx, Adalbert, 66
Michel, Albert, 81–84
Morla, Víctor, 17

Author Index

Moyise, Steve, 91
Müller, Møgens, 65
Muñoz Iglesias, Salvador, 84

Newman, Hillel I., 22
Nongbri, Brent, 71
Norton, Gerard J., 23

Origen, 2, 5, 7, 14, 19–23, 27–28, 33, 49–53, 76, 85, 94–96, 99
Orlinsky, Harry M., 14

Pammachius, 34, 41
Pamphilus, 2
Paul VI, Pope, 108
Petersen, William L., 66
Philo of Alexandria, 58, 75
Piquer Otero, Andrés, 101–2
Pius X, Pope, 107
Plato, 33–34
Ptolemy, King of Alexandria 33–34, 48, 54, 59

Rahlfs, Alfred, 49, 69, 71
Roberts, Colin H., 71
Rusen-Weinhold, Ulrich, 49

Schenker, Adrian, 99
Segal, Michael, 15
Seijas de los Ríos, Guadalupe, 86
Sgherri, Giuseppe, 19
Shedinger, Robert F., 66
Skeat, Theodore C., 71

Sophronius, 31
Steyn, Gert J., 49
Sunnia, 22
Symmachus, 2, 7, 10, 19–22, 30, 41, 49, 55, 69

Tatian, 66
Taylor, Charles, 20
Tertullian, 16
Theodotion, 2, 7, 14–15, 19–22, 30, 41, 49, 53, 55, 68–69, 76–77
Theodulf, bishop of Orleans, 88
Toloni, Giancarlo, 18
Torijano Morales, Pablo, 101–2
Tov, Emanuel, 13, 44, 99, 100, 102
Trapè, Agostino, 94
Troyer, Kristin de, 13, 101

Urassa, Wenceslaus M., 91

Vaccari, Alberto, 22
Veltri, Giuseppe, 46, 53, 61, 63, 95, 102–3

Wagner, J. Ross, 50, 65
Walton, Brian, 97
Wasserstein, Abraham, 44, 75
Wasserstein, David J., 44, 75
Weber, Robert, 107
Weis, Richard D., 101
Wright, Benjamin G., 17

Ziegler, Joseph, 13, 69

Scripture Index

HEBREW BIBLE / OLD TESTAMENT

Genesis	34, 51
4:7	37
12:3	61
14:17–20	48
22:18	61

Exodus	51
3:14	58

Numbers

11:16	55

Deuteronomy

4:34	37
26:8	37

Joshua	13, 101

Ruth	77

1–2 Samuel	26

1 Samuel

2:1–10	13

16–18	13
23:11–12	37

1–2 Kings	26, 101

1–2 Chronicles	27–28, 40

Nehemiah

11:25–35	13

Esther	81–82

Job	13–15, 23, 29, 51
14:4	57

Psalms	48, 50, 87, 89, 91–91, 110
2	54, 56
8	66
8:4–6	48
8:6	91, 110
16:8–11	46, 61
16:10	46, 91
40	112
40:6–8	48
40:7–9	49
40:7–8	113
40:7 (LXX 39:7)	49–50, 91

Scripture Index

(Psalms continued)

45:6-7	48
82:1	110
89:7	110
95:7-11	48
97:7	110
102:25-27	48
110:1	48, 91
110:3	91
110:4	48
138:1	110
145	38-39

Proverbs

18:4	33
22:28	52

Songs 77

Isaiah 34, 80, 94

6:9-10	40
7:14	18, 21, 41, 61, 68, 70, 110, 113
9:5	73
31:9	32
42:1	73
53:2	33, 73
64:4	33

Jeremiah 10-12, 51, 94, 98, 101

Lamentations 77

Ezekiel 13

2:1-2a	11
25	11
27:1	11
33:14-26	11
39:4-13	11

Daniel 15-17, 76, 81-82

4-6	15
7-8	15
3:24-90	16, 51

Hosea 30

11:1	33-34

Amos

6:5	32

Zechariah

12:10	7, 33, 68

APOCRYPHAL / DEUTEROCANONICAL

Tobit 3, 16-18, 77-78

Judith 3, 16

Esther, Greek Additions 16-17, 51, 81

Wisdom 16, 57-58, 62, 79

2:1	58
2:21	58
2:22	58
5:6	58
6-9	58
7:17	58

Scripture Index

Sirach	16–17, 62, 77–78
Baruch	16, 62
Letter of Jeremiah	16
Susanna (Dan 13)	16, 50
Bel and the Dragon (Dan 14)	16, 51
1 Maccabees	16, 62
2 Maccabees	16, 62, 79

PSEUDEPIGRAPHA

3 Ezra	77
4 Esd	
14	53
14:21–22	53

NEW TESTAMENT

Matthew	40, 106
1:22–23	68
1:23	61, 69–70, 110
2:15	33
2:23	33
13:14–15	40–41
23:2–3	54
Mark	106
Luke	106
John	
7:38	33
19:37	7, 33, 68
Acts	
2:22–36	46
2:25–31	61
3:25	61
1 Corinthians	
2:9	33
12:28–30	35
Galatians	
3:8–9	61
Hebrews	50, 113
2:5–9	110
5:5–7	48
10:1–10	112
10:4–7	49
10:5–7	112
10:5	49–50
10:6	49

DEAD SEA SCROLLS

1QIs^a	70, 73, 108
1QIs^b	108
4QJosh^a	101
4QJr^b	12
4QJr^d	12
11QPs^a	38

8ḤevXIIgr　　　　　45, 68

RABBINIC WRITINGS
Misnah
Avot

1　　　　　　　　　　　55

Babylonian Talmud
Berakhot

5a.3　　　　　　　　　　55

Megillah

9a　　　　　　　　　　　75

OTHER RABBINIC WORKS
Megillat Taanit

50　　　　　　　　　　　32

Sefer Torah

I:8–9　　　　　　　　　　32

www.ingramcontent.com/pod-product-compliance
Lightning Source LLC
Chambersburg PA
CBHW070916160426
43193CB00011B/1478